T0348713

The Fractional CMO Method

Attract, Convert and Serve High-Paying Clients on Your Terms

CASEY STANTON

Foreword by Parris Lampropoulos

The Fractional CMO Method
Attract, Convert and Serve High-Paying Clients on Your Terms

All Rights Reserved

COPYRIGHT © 2022 Casey Stanton

This book may not be reproduced, transmitted, or stored in whole or in part by any means, including graphic, electronic, or mechanical, without the express written consent of the publisher except in the case of brief questions embodied in critical articles and reviews.

ISBN:
Paperback - 978-1-954759-70-1
Hardcover - 978-1-954759-71-8
eBook - 978-1-954759-69-5

Cranberry Press Publish

Download the Fractional CMO Toolkit for Free

READ THIS FIRST

As a *thank you* for reading my book, I would like to give you the Fractional CMO Toolkit to get you armed to win clients and serve them quickly... absolutely FREE.

Go to **CMOx.co/toolkit** to claim yours now!

What People Are Saying

"In this book, Casey Stanton provides a roadmap for becoming a Fractional CMO along with valuable wisdom and perspective for companies looking to make that same hire in their business."

– Ryan Levesque
CEO of The ASK Method® Company

"This may be the fastest way to add 6-figures to your income as a marketer! Casey shares what it takes to become an in-demand fractional CMO and diversify your income by serving multiple clients."

– Josh Nelson
Author of "The Seven Figure Agency Roadmap"

When Casey Stanton speaks, I sit up and listen. Heck, I'll even "shush" the room if I have to. Because he's not only incredibly smart, but he has a unique ability to take complex ideas and distill them into very actionable steps. Which, as a creative, I need if I'm actually going to get something done. Beyond being a brilliant thinker and communicator though, Casey's greatest assets are his vast experience (the man's been through the entrepreneurial ringer and come out wiser and more polished), and, most importantly, his genuine caring for other people. I've never seen him hold back "the goods" in any setting - whether on a barstool, a microphone, or leading a group. Finally, we have one convenient place for all of his hard won wisdom, and it's right here in The Fractional CMO Method. If you have any plans to market your skills - and don't want to get swallowed up by the (ever-increasing) competition, or abused by bad clients, you've got to devour this book right away.

– Kevin Rogers
Founder of Copy Chief

"The Fractional CMO Method helps transform marketers into chief marketing officers -- a vital role needed by today's process-driven companies. Casey shares how to build and lead a marketing team in order to predictably achieve ambitious revenue outcomes. I particularly appreciate his model of success at the intersection of Income, Impact, and Freedom - that is the essence of what's important for an entrepreneurial company."

– Mark C. Winters
Co-Author of "Rocket Fuel"

"There's an emerging model where fast-growth organizations are bringing in fractional CFOs and CMOs... those companies have greater flexibility and often beat incumbents in the marketplace. Casey leads the charge for fractional CMOs. If you're considering offering fractional CMO services, read this book and learn from the best."

– Vinnie Fisher
Founder, Fully Accountable

"Marketing tactics without a robust strategy is a waste. Businesses more than ever before need someone to build their marketing strategy and lead their team. Casey shows you how to do exactly that as a fractional CMO in this book!"

– Joel Erway
Author of "High Ticket Courses"

"I don't follow leaders without scars on their face. Casey has his scars, won through the years inside over a hundred businesses. What he shares in this book will help any ambitious marketer declare themselves CMO and serve clients with confidence."

– Bo Eason
NFL All-Pro, In-Demand Speaker & 8-Time Best-Selling Author

"Casey's book is a game changer for marketing professionals wanting to make more money in less time. The Fractional CMO Method turns short term clients into long lasting relationships built on a foundation of value."

– Leon Kolaski
Agency Owner

"Casey took what feels like an overwhelming topic and made it so simple. I honestly can't remember the last time I was sitting on the edge of my seat reading a business book. Seriously. There's a lot of talk right now about the CMO world and what a great opportunity it is (and can be). But where do you start? How do you start? How do you transition from what you're already doing to going down this path? Well, Casey answers this and so much more throughout the book. And it's totally relatable. What can feel like a very overwhelming task is broken down into very simple, measurable steps that I believe pretty much anyone can follow."

– Rory F. Stern, PsyD
Founder, RFS Digital Media, LLC

"I spent years managing and directing marketing teams, so I thought the transition to being a fractional CMO would have been easy. Unfortunately, it wasn't. I spent years grinding away, and eventually burning out before realizing I had to make a change.

After reading Casey's book, I can see exactly why things went wrong. I can't help but think that if I had the framework and system that Casey shares in this book, those early years into the transition would have been so much easier.

Casey's Fractional CMO Method is simple, smart, and a complete win-win for both you (the Fractional CMO) and your future clients.

I can't recommend this book (and Casey's teachings) enough if you're looking for a smart way to work with your future clients. Save yourself a bunch of heartbreak and hassle, and avoid the biggest pitfalls of over-servicing demanding clients. This system is a great way to amplify your income and impact by doing your best work for great clients who love you."

– Ross O'Lochlainn
Founder of Conversion Engineering

"I've helped hundreds of companies by staffing them with virtual and executive assistants. Often these hires are forced to run marketing campaigns without a larger strategy in place. The Fractional CMO Method lays out how a marketer can become a fractional CMO and fill the much-needed gap in businesses today: the role of the marketing strategist and leader"

– Trivinia Barber
Founder of PriorityVA

Foreword

I have a confession to make.

Although I am best known as a copywriter, the reality is that most of my income does *not* come from writing copy. It comes from being a Fractional CMO.

In fact, last year I made *three times* as much money being a CMO than I did as a copywriter.

And if you are currently a copywriter, agency owner, or other marketing professional, there's a good chance you can make more money, too.

In this book, Casey Stanton shows you exactly how to do it.

He shows you how to take all the knowledge and skills you have now and leverage them so that you have multiple streams of income.

He shows you how to create a pipeline of potential clients so that you can decide which ones to take on and which ones to let go.

And he gives you a simple framework that lets you diagnose your clients' top problems… come up with the solutions… and then delegate the actual implementation of those solutions.

That last part is important. If you're like most marketing professionals, you're currently getting paid for "doing the thing." Maybe you're creating funnels. Maybe you're buying media. Maybe you're writing Facebook ads. You're getting paid to do the thing, and you're throwing in marketing strategy for free.

I used to be in the "doing" trap, too. I spent my days toiling over sales copy. Then one day, I got the idea to hire and train other copywriters. I fired myself as chief copywriter… and hired myself as copy chief. And it was one of the greatest days of my life.

Now that I no longer had to write the copy myself, I had spare time. And I decided to take some of that spare time and do consulting, a.k.a. getting paid to flap my lips.

And over time, this morphed into being a Fractional CMO.

Getting here took a lot of trial and error. I made a lot of mistakes along the way. But you don't have to make those same mistakes. That's because Casey provides you with a clear blueprint on how to get the positive results without the pitfalls.

He shows you what qualities to look for in a potential client… plus the red flags that should make you run the other way. He shows you how to find A-players to do the work for you and how to avoid B- and C-players. He shows you how to set boundaries so that clients aren't calling you on evenings and weekends.

If you'd like to make more money while working less and creating greater impact, then I urge you to read on.

Parris Lampropoulos

Contents

Acknowledgements

I am a byproduct of the incredible people in my life who have given me guidance, support and encouragement.

A deep bow of gratitude to Eugene Schwartz, Claude Hopkins, David Ogilvy, Gary Halbert, Dan Kennedy, Gary Bencivenga and Eben Pagan whom I have had the pleasure of studying through their generous contributions to our field of marketing.

David in Royal Oak, thank you for giving me my first break. Derek Freund for the gift of being in your GKIC chapter well before I could afford the membership fee, and for allowing me to read from your library.

Richard, thank you for your continual mentoring and insights. Our calls are invaluable.

To all the great executives I've had the honor of supporting, thank you for leading by example and trusting me to support you.

To my mastermind crew Sean, Erika, Geordie, Ben, Josh and Melaine. Thank you for ensuring I stay well-rounded in my personal life and business. It's always a good day when we get to catch up.

To Bill, the truest of homies. Thank you for your encouragement, support, memes and calling me out on my bullshit. I wouldn't have written this book if it wasn't for you.

To my family who have always encouraged me to be who I am.

To my team: Hannah, Nibir, Jon, Tim, Edgar - y'all make this more fun and rewarding than I could ask for. I'm humbled by your continual effort to grow, to serve a greater audience, and to do it all while having a great time.

Raphael, I am forever grateful for your support, commitment and belief in what we're building.

And finally, I acknowledge the sacrifices you've made, Adelaide, to allow me to build this business and write this book. The long nights, the weekends of work, the travel, and the ups-and-downs; you've allowed me to have both the life of my dreams and a business I'm proud of. Thank you.

Dedication

This book is for every marketer who knows they were born to do something great and leave their mark on the world.

Introduction

This book is your roadmap for building a Fractional CMO practice that can generate $500,000 a year or more.

That's a half-a-million dollars a year with you working less than 40 hours a week, from anywhere in the world.

Sounds impossible? If you're an agency owner, marketing director, freelancer, marketing consultant, in-house marketer, or even a VP of marketing, you can follow the steps I lay out in this book to start winning clients that **each** pay $3,000 to $15,000 a month *or more*. You can even win a client *on the side* that you can serve in a couple hours a month.

The U.S. Small Business Administration has published that there are over 31.7 *million* small and medium-sized businesses (SMBs) in the United States alone and many of them are in desperate need of a Fractional CMO.

If you follow the method I'm about to share with you, you'll have a clear path to attract, convert and serve your ideal clients with confidence.

My story of becoming a successful Fractional CMO was a bigger rollercoaster than Frodo's journey through Middle-earth.

I was able to quickly build my revenue up to $23,000 a month and felt like I had made it.

Then one day, I lost it all. And I mean *everything*.

Through perseverance, **I rebuilt my Fractional CMO practice to $46,500 in cash collected each month** while working 30 hours a week and fixed the problems that allowed my business to fall apart.

Hitting rock bottom hurts. Seeing my wife's face when I told her we lost *another* client and I didn't know how we'd make rent forever changed me. It changed our marriage.

I decided at that moment, sitting in an Airbnb in Bala Cynwyd just outside of Philadelphia, Pennsylvania, that I would never put my family in that position again.

In this book, I will share with you how I built my Fractional CMO practice, the weaknesses that allowed the business to collapse, and the step-by-step approach I followed to build an antifragile Fractional CMO practice to more than a half million dollars a year.

I promise you that if you heed what I share, you'll win more business, serve it with less stress, create world-class outcomes for your clients, build a reputation as the *right person* for the job, and make the income *and* impact you desire.

Let's get into it…

The 3 Biggest Challenges as a Fractional CMO

When you make the decision to be a Fractional CMO, you'll be faced with three big challenges. The small challenges like bookkeeping, taxes, health insurance, and website hosting are easy to solve. But without a plan to overcome these three big challenges, you'll live a feast-or-famine life, feeling stressed and exhausted during anemic months.

The first big challenge you'll face as a Fractional CMO is:

You must have control over your pipeline.

When I started as a Fractional CMO, I got lucky. A friend of mine had a buddy who wanted to grow his information and coaching business. After sharing my desire to get into the world of Fractional CMO services, my buddy introduced me to his friend, and I made the sale.

That first sale was life-changing. Not because it was the biggest package I had ever sold, but because I was going to take the whole fee. When I worked at a marketing agency, I would make 45% of my consulting fees. This sale alone doubled my typical rate!

I was on cloud nine as the client signed the proposal and funded the project. I knew I could scale the business and serve a few more clients in a similar capacity, but the problem quickly became clear:

I didn't have a pipeline.

Word of mouth isn't scalable.

My friend who had made the introduction didn't have any other connections with business owners that needed a Fractional CMO.

I found myself in a compromised position as I made my plans to leave the marketing agency. The agency paid me each and every pay period, without fail. But leaving the agency and being able to enjoy the entire fee I charged meant I was solely responsible for bringing in new business.

When a lead would come to me, I found myself bending in every direction to find a way to sell and service them. It was OK if they just needed me to run Google Ads, right? Maybe I could hire someone on Upwork and have them build the client a website... I could do anything, or so I thought.

The work I was doing was all new, custom, and unique. There was no increased efficiency over time. Everything was hard. Every time I met with a lead, or a client, I had to *invent* the next thing to do.

This is when the second big challenge bubbled up:

I wasn't getting the results my clients needed.

It's embarrassing to even admit it. I'm sure you and I are similar: Lock me in a room with a problem to solve and a computer and I'll figure out the solution. I'll read the books. I'll think critically. I'll "walk around" the problem and come up with a great solution.

But that effort takes *time*.

It reminded me of a sales call while working at the marketing agency. I was in a sales role and pitched a prospect on a website build. In the end, they turned down the proposal. Out of curiosity, I asked them why they said no, and the reply dramatically changed how I saw the work I was doing. They said:

"While you're obviously smart and hardworking, you've never done this before. We think we'd be better off working with someone who has done this before."

That got my attention!

I prided myself on being able to get my clients results, no matter their niche, marketing department make-up, or offering. It was clear that in *every situation,* there was a better marketer than me.

Could I figure out how to rewrite title tags and suggest new H1 tags for a webpage? Sure.

Could I build a Facebook Ads account and start driving traffic? Yep.

But I didn't have benchmarks. I didn't have a track record of success in a specific niche.

The solutions I gave to clients were good, but not great. They were certainly *not* the kind of outcomes that build a reputation as the "go-to" marketer for hire.

The third big challenge that I faced was that:

My contracts were short-lived.

If you've ever sold marketing consulting before, you know the revolving door of:

- Prospecting
- Selling
- Closing
- Servicing
- Spinning-down

It's an infinite loop. Just as you close a new client, you get a notice from another that your contract is ending. Any joy that you have in hitting a new monthly income target quickly disappears when you experience anemic months.

If you've been on an income rollercoaster, you know how hard it is to plan *anything* in life.

One great month can convince you that you *can* build a great lifestyle, only to lose hope the next month as you take money out of savings to pay your mortgage.

Boundaries are also hard to keep. When you're hungry, you're willing to work nights and weekends. When you're full up on clients, you're racked with fear of losing them and take calls outside of your normal working hours to keep them satisfied.

You can easily find yourself working every day, at all hours. Your phone blows up with Slack notifications. You read each and every email. You can claim that you have freedom, but do you <u>really</u>?

I decided that if I was going to build a business where I was in control of my income… if I was going to build a business where I could make an incredible impact on the world… if I was going to have the lifestyle I wanted of being a present father and husband and still enjoy hobbies and a social life, then I needed to solve these three challenges once and for all.

After all, if work doesn't provide the lifestyle you want and if life isn't fun, then what's the point?

The Fractional CMO Method™

When you treat your career as a business, you start to see where there is room for lasting improvement and systems.

The three problems I set out to solve were:

1. Complete control over my pipeline
2. Creating incredible results for my clients
3. Having long-term clients that I loved working with

For you to be a successful Fractional CMO who doesn't rely on *luck* alone, you need:

- Hot lead flow
- An effortless way to sell the leads
- Service and delegation confidence

In the next few chapters, I'll break these out for you in clear, actionable ways so you can get to work and start building your Fractional CMO practice.

You may be wondering who I am and why you should trust me. Please don't let me convince you of anything. My goal is to share my story and experience of helping myself and other marketers grow their income by landing $3,000 to $15,000 per month Fractional CMO clients. If this makes sense to you and you believe becoming a Fractional CMO is a worthy pursuit in your life, I share further in the book ready-to-use templates and training to get you started.

I also have a private group of Fractional CMOs that I personally coach and train to build their practices and become the leader in their niche. If that's interesting to you, flip to the last chapter in the book to learn more.

CHAPTER 1

The 3 Lessons in Becoming a Fractional CMO

O n a sunny spring afternoon in 2008, I donned my green cap and gown and made my way to the Breslin Center at Michigan State University to receive my undergraduate degree.

While everyone around me was excited and ready to walk across the stage and receive their diploma, I was frozen.

I knew the moment that I was handed my diploma, I would be officially catapulted into the *real world* where I had to get a full-time job and take care of myself.

You must remember what the spring of 2008 was like… it was the start of the United States housing crisis. Over the next few months, friends and family members found themselves out of a job while the economy fell into recession.

Any hope I had for an easy entrance into the labor market was quickly crushed as those with PhDs fought for jobs in retail.

I made the decision many of my friends had to make: to move back home with my parents.

I found work mowing lawns in northern Michigan. After a week of silence on the back of the mowers, I decided I needed to get myself off the mower and into something more *rewarding*… but I didn't know what that was.

The local library had copies of Tony Robbins's books as well as Dan Kennedy's *The Ultimate Sales Letter*. With an iPod full of new education, I committed to finding my way out of mowing.

One afternoon, I pulled the work truck up to the home, nestled twenty feet back from the shore of Lake Michigan, of a man named Dave. His home was striking; he had a luxury car, a house with big windows overlooking the lake, and a perfectly cut lawn. Something about his home resonated with me, and it was all I could think about that day.

"What did Dave do? How does he have such a beautiful home? How could I have a home like that?!"

The following week, after mowing and edging his lawn, I was packing up to leave.

Dave was just returning from an afternoon out.

While he was walking to his front door, he stopped to chat.

Without much tact, I asked him, "Dave, you have a beautiful home. How did you do it?"

Surprised, Dave teetered back on his heels and took a breath. Then he leaned in and opened up. He shared that he had invented a product, manufactured it, and had a group of distributors and salespeople who sold his product.

Coming from an IBM family, I had never really thought about entrepreneurship. In high school and college, I offered my services as a magician for birthday and cocktail parties, as a bartender, and even cleaned toilets at three different jobs, but I never considered myself an entrepreneur.

Dave opened my eyes to a whole new possibility: I didn't have to exist in someone else's organization as a full-time worker. I could invent. I could take control of my livelihood.

After probing Dave with more questions, I felt I had overstayed my welcome. I strapped down my mower and blower and thanked Dave, then headed back to the depot.

It was another night where all I could think about was Dave's success and how he didn't have a master's degree or any specialized schooling.

The following week, after I had mowed Dave's property, I knocked on his door. Dave greeted me and I asked him directly: "Dave, I'd love to sell your product. Can you front me a few units?"

Despite my eagerness, he declined. He said I had to purchase the units just like all of his dealers. The following week, I scraped up enough to buy a box of his widgets and set out to sell them.

Sales were easy for me. The first door I knocked, I made more profit than I did the previous week mowing lawns! Instantly, I knew I was on to something...

Another market condition of 2008 was the record-high gas prices. My Jeep and the long distances between homes in my rural hometown of northern Michigan, as well as a little laziness, helped me realize that I could sell Dave's products online and never have to spend a dollar on gas.

I dove head-first into copywriting, PPC, SEO, website building on Dreamweaver. I did whatever I could to sell these products online. And the result? Zero sales.

I couldn't sell a single one.

Turns out, the product wasn't that desirable and I had just been lucky in my neighborhood.

I took that energy and looked for the next product to sell. I stumbled into a man in the information publishing industry and he made me an offer: $1,000 a month to run his Google Ads. Quickly, I learned the ropes and had successful campaigns on Google, Bing and Yahoo Ads.

My client was based in the Detroit area and I was four hours away. Knowing that he only cared about my work outcomes, I set sail on a 4-month bicycle trip from Madrid to Rome. I had no idea how I would get from Madrid to Rome and I gave myself plenty of time to figure it out. Along the way, I'd stop in internet cafes to make updates to the ad campaigns, write new creatives and add negative keywords.

This was my first lesson as a Fractional CMO:

> Business owners want outcomes, not labor. If I focus on big problems and solve them, I can get rewarded for the solution, not for the time it took me to solve the problem.

This was addicting.

After returning from Europe, I set up my one-man marketing consultancy in Ann Arbor, Michigan, renting a slab of concrete in my sister's basement. My bedroom door was a curtain and my headboard was the furnace. It was all I could afford with my meager wages, but it was enough to let me focus on building my expertise.

While at a bar, I bumped into a marketing agency owner and we hit it off. A trip to Burning Man later, I started contracting with his agency. From there, I began thinking about where I wanted to live as my livelihood was not predicated on my location.

I found myself in New Orleans, after taking advice from a traveling yoga DJ while in Nashville.

In New Orleans, I worked long, hard hours for a marketing agency. I helped clients sell millions of dollars of products through Jeff Walker's Product Launch Formula. I helped Peter Diamandis raise $1.5M on Kickstarter for a space telescope. Feeling like I had found my footing as a marketer, I looked at the universities in the area for an MBA program that would help me level up.

I scrutinized the syllabus for the MBA program and found the classes to be lacking. Universities were not teaching digital marketing, and if they were, they weren't talking about the efficacy of a one-click upsell, or a free-plus-shipping offer. In an effort to give back, I reached out to the department head and asked if I could guest lecture for a class.

That guest lecture turned into a position at Tulane University where I served as an Adjunct Professor of Marketing for three years. I loved teaching students how to approach marketing in a way that is clear, measurable, and approachable.

But after three years, I longed for something else.

My girlfriend and I sold our belongings, bought an SUV and hitched up an RV. We set out for a three-year adventure across the US and Canada to find the perfect place to live. We called this adventure "City Dating." Halfway through the trip, we got married in Nashville.

The Stress of Working in an Agency

Despite ticking off those huge milestones in my personal life, I still found myself regularly exhausted from working at the marketing agency. The constant demands from multiple clients— the late-night calls when a funnel broke… launches that happened on every major holiday… It became too much and I grew tired of the urgency of everything.

My wife encouraged me to leave the agency, but I didn't know what I'd do.

I didn't want to polish my resume. I didn't want to apply on Indeed.

I wanted to be my own boss. I wanted to become deadly at what I was doing!

So I went to a coffee shop and thought long and hard about what I wanted to do and who I wanted to be.

Over a latte, I realized **the second lesson as a Fractional CMO**:

> I need to *position myself* to be the trusted advisor who can find big problems, then solve them.

While working at the marketing agency, I was regularly pulled into sales calls where prospects would have a problem that needed to be solved. Shopping cart integrations, data warehousing, product launches, and more. As I reflected at the coffee shop, I saw the well of possibilities spring from the well of sales conversations.

It's hard to admit, but I'm not much of an inventor. I have never had a great idea for a new product. I've never been one to come up with the next gadget or SaaS idea. As such, I needed to put myself in spaces with those who had a wellspring of invention and innovation.

Leaving the marketing agency meant leaving the faucet of opportunity.

I knew that in order to be successful for the rest of my life, I needed to position myself where opportunities were plentiful. I couldn't compete on the open market like everyone else; I had to take control of my pipeline.

But where is that fountainhead?

Again, I found myself without a clear plan. I knew something was wrong… I knew there was a better way… but I didn't know what to do.

Around that time, I was able to close my second client as a Fractional CMO. My wife knew I was onto something, but I was hesitant to agree. See, this second client came from another lucky connection. A colleague of mine had introduced me to a company and I had won the deal. My income at this point was 50% more than I had ever been paid at the marketing agency but my confidence was lower than ever.

What would happen if I lost a client?

Eek!

Motivated by "fear of loss," I poured my heart and soul into serving my clients. It became abundantly clear that while I was only working 10 hours a week per client, I was spending an equal amount of time figuring out what to do with the clients! My late-night stress and anxiety, mixed with desperate phone calls to friends and my network, allowed me to keep the contract alive one month at a time.

I didn't know if I would be in the penthouse or the doghouse next month.

With a little more luck, I brought in a third client.

From the outside, everything looked great. I had a great income of $23,000 a month. I had just hired a US-based executive assistant to support me in serving my clients.

But the pain behind the surface was real:

… would I lose everything?

… would I be able to make payroll?

In January, I flew out to see my biggest client. I had been working with them for a few months and aimed to get them to commit to a 12-month contract which would alleviate my fears.

Everything went according to plan. I presented my strategy to the CEO and the board. The Chairman liked it. The CEO and I met outside after the meeting and he shook my hand. He said:

"Casey, that was great. We're excited to work with you for the year and hopefully beyond!"

I texted my wife in elation as I walked the cemetery behind the office building where Hugh Hefner, Marilyn Monroe and Rodney Danger-field are buried.

Later that day, I flew home with a pep in my step. I knew I had just solved the biggest issue plaguing me, my business, and my family.

About two weeks later, the contract was up for formal renewal. I received a call from the CEO. He skipped the niceties and went straight for the news:

"Casey, I'm sorry to share this but we will not be renewing your con-tract. Today is your last day."

Shellshocked, I stammered, "Wha...wha...what do you mean? We had a deal."

A moment later I learned that the Chairman had disliked the overall approach the CEO had made for the growth of the company and the Chairman had fired the CEO, CMO (me), CFO, and COO.

In one fell swoop, I lost half my income.

Down but not out, I licked my wounds and kept serving my other two clients. I walked my dog through the golf course near our rental in Bala Cynwyd thinking about how I'd go win a new client and get our revenue up.

A week later, my biggest remaining client decided to stop working together. Our contract had come up for renewal and they didn't believe I could continue providing value for them. I had a 7-day notice that my income was dropping *again*.

At this point, all I had left was one client paying me $2,500 a month. That wasn't enough to cover rent, food, the debt we owed on our wed-ding, and my assistant.

If you've ever experienced a similar downturn, you know just how awful it feels. It's as if the world collapses around you. Not only was I broke, but I also had to tell my assistant whom I valued that I had to cut him back from full-time hours.

A waterfall of emotions would wash over me throughout the day.

Realizing that I had no pipeline meant I had no way of winning business.

I had given up on prospecting because I was sure the California client was as good as closed. I didn't have a plan to replace my other client. My savings account was dry.

$2 Lean Cuisine Meals Refocused Me

I remember it like it was yesterday: Grabbing the flier at the entrance to the supermarket to find coupons and spending twice as much time as I ever had shopping for food. I would buy my wife Amy's Kitchen frozen meals and pick up $2 Lean Cuisines for myself.

Eating those TV dinners in our rental was a constant reminder that while I was a good marketer, I wasn't good at running a business.

I would waffle between second-guessing myself and recommitting myself to whatever it would take to become successful again.

I grabbed a pen and paper and got to work.

I knew I needed to be positioned as a trusted advisor, but I couldn't keep doing what I was doing. It was too hectic. The context switching of serving a company in fintech in the morning then insurance in the afternoon, then a health-and-fitness in the evening was jarring and unsustainable. Any wins I had with one client couldn't be applied to the other.

I burned more time just trying to figure out what to do than actually doing the work.

This led to me realizing the third lesson as a Fractional CMO:

Focus on a specific problem type and get really good at solving it.

Another way to say this is to choose a niche. But a niche isn't the only way to do it. Instead of choosing a niche, I realized I could develop a process to serve companies where any win with one could be ethically applied to another.

How a 94-Year-Old Billionaire Changed Everything for Me

My underlying principle came from a 1990's speech by billionaire and vice chairman of Berkshire Hathaway, Charles Munger, who said:

"Well, the first rule is that you can't really know anything if you just remember isolated facts and try and bang 'em back. If the facts don't hang together on a latticework of theory, you don't have them in a usable form. **You've got to have models in your head.** And you've got to array your experience both vicarious and direct on this latticework of models. You may have noticed students who just try to remember and pound back what is remembered. Well, they fail in school and in life. **You've got to hang experience on a latticework of models in your head.**"

I needed to develop a model to serve clients as their Fractional CMO.

The model had to:

- Help identify the biggest problems to solve
- Create a structure in which to solve them where I do not have to be the expert of *everything*
- Generate the biggest value for my clients
- ... and most importantly, provide a consistent approach I could take to *all* my clients without extreme preparation

18

The idea of developing a framework is what made the biggest shift for me.

If I had a framework, I could work with clients for whom I could apply the framework.

If a prospect came to me that had a problem I couldn't solve with the framework, I simply would not take them on as a client.

A framework would simplify my work, keep me in a position of confidence, and, I bet, help me create a long-lasting relationship with my clients where I delivered value month after month, without fail.

Later in this book, I'll share with you what I created: The Functional Marketing® Framework.

You'll see first-hand how to apply it to serve your clients and simplify your work, all while making bigger and bigger outcomes for your clients.

Sharing the Success

Today, my life is much different than it was in Bala Cynwyd. I have had the opportunity to serve incredible clients as their Fractional CMO and I love the work. Every week, I can see myself getting smarter and better at building my clients' businesses. My income has soared.

Upon reflection, one thing that was missing in my life was the joy I experienced in helping others. While teaching at Tulane University, I enjoyed refining my ideas and supporting my students in the classroom. I still keep in touch with many of my students and it brings me such satisfaction to see them continue to excel in their careers.

That's when I decided that I wanted to share what I had built as a Fractional CMO.

Every time I solved a problem a *second* time for a client, I had my assistant build a Standard Operating Procedure. These SOPs allowed me to deliver great results to my clients without having to reinvent the wheel. As my SOP library started to swell in size, I started receiving interest from other marketers who wanted to join my company.

Here's the problem: Fractional CMOs want to be their own boss. They didn't want to report to me. They wanted to do their own thing, in their own way, but with the tools and approach I had proven to be successful.

That's why I created the CMOx Accelerator. I now personally coach marketing consultants, agency owners, SVPs of Marketing, and in-house marketing folks to reinvent themselves as a Fractional CMO, work with great companies and propel themselves to the next tax bracket.

If you're interested in learning more, my team is available to answer your questions. Just go to CMOx.co/grow

Artificial Constraints

When my wife, our dog Pepper, and I lived in our 28' Coachmen Freedom Express travel trailer, I had inadvertently created artificial constraints in my life. As I grew my Fractional CMO practice, I was limited by my environment.

WiFi at campgrounds was awful.

Cell service was spotty.

I was never anywhere I could be on-video reliably.

Writing my first-ever job post to hire an Executive Assistant from our 28' Coachmen Freedom Express RV while parked at the Washington / Pittsburgh KOA campground. In the picture is our kitchenette, my office, our couch with our street mutt Pepper, and Diet 7Up, the greatest drink to ever be created

Instead of being frustrated, I leaned into these constraints and realized that once we had found our city to move to, I would have new constraints: having a baby.

Knowing that we wanted to have a family, I focused on something so simple and fundamental, it was surprising I had never done it before. I guess I was just caught up in the day-to-day life working at the agency.

My mission became to create a future where I could be anywhere in the world, solve big problems and be paid well for my work. I didn't want to have to fly from stage to stage, speaking for a living. I didn't want to have to be on video calls every single day. I didn't want to have dozens of team members that I had to manage, all while bringing in business for them as a marketing agency. I just wanted to deliver a lot of value in a focused way, optimizing for impact and therefore my income.

Odds are, you're in the same position that I was, thinking about your career and trajectory in marketing.

One thing that became clear to me was that the highest ascension in marketing is to be the Chief Marketing Officer.

If I was going to be in a position to solve the biggest marketing problems, I had to position myself as a CMO.

If there is any good news that came out of the COVID-19 pandemic, it's that the hiring landscape has forever changed. Companies that previously would have never considered hiring a remote CMO are now operating their company with a mix of remote and in-office team members.

Further, these small and medium-sized businesses are in greater need than ever before of comprehensive, effective marketing.

This is truly a perfect storm for us marketers. By taking action and declaring yourself as a Fractional CMO, then serving your clients to achieve new heights, we're in a blue ocean.

Moonlight, Get a Client "On the Side" or Go All In – It's Your Choice

If you're a full-time employee and you're considering leaving your employment to be a Fractional CMO, you can reduce your risk and pick up one single client and try it out. If you work on the east coast of the US, you can serve a west coast Fractional CMO client after 5:00 p.m. Eastern without any issue.

If you own an agency, it's likely you've been giving away marketing strategies *for free* in order to sell your agency services. You've had to come up with a complete marketing strategy for a client just so you can deploy an ad campaign or build them a new website. Instead of giving away the strategy for free, you can make marketing strategy and leadership its own profit center as a Fractional CMO.

Even more, as an agency owner, you'll get to dig deeper with clients as a Fractional CMO than you ever could have with your agency before. That means when you uncover problems that your agency can solve, you are able to serve your clients deeper and faster.

When I was an in-house marketer at the agency, I regularly made my agency a *lot* of money. If you're an in-house marketer and want to break free of your agency or employer, the answer is *not* to bring $500–$1,000 a month projects on the side. You need a repeatable, dependable way to serve a single client or two that pays you $3,000 a month or more.

At the start, closing my first Fractional CMO client forever changed my view on my abilities and what was possible for myself.

You might be thinking, *"Maybe this Fractional CMO thing has some merit."*

Before you commit yourself to becoming a Fractional CMO, first, let's get clear on who you are, what you want in your career, and see if there are any shortcuts to get you there…

Wyatt's story should be able to give you a better insight regarding these considerations.

Successful Agency Owner Becomes Fractional CMO to Go Deeper

Wyatt Chambers is a successful agency owner based in Tucson, Arizona with over 100 clients, who wanted to get back to the fun stuff in marketing: strategy.

I love Wyatt's story because he was a very successful agency owner who just wanted *more*. For years, he's run his marketing agency and has a systematic way to attract and serve clients. He built his business, hired a large staff and ran the agency as CEO. The problem was, he found himself wishing he could dig deeper with a few clients and really revolutionize what they were doing.

Wyatt also knew one of his weaknesses was standard operating procedures (SOPs). Having SOPs would mean he and his team could consistently produce better work products for their clients and reduce the human capital needed to accomplish their client's goals. Better results in less time are exactly what any agency needs.

When Wyatt joined the CMOx Accelerator, he gave himself a simple goal: to win one new client a quarter. This way, he could be very choosy and find the best client for himself and for his agency. The second part of his goal was really exciting for me to hear. Wyatt wanted to work his way into new businesses where he could identify big problems and create marketing strategies to overcome them with the labor of his agency.

Six months into the CMOx Accelerator, Wyatt already has two long-term fractional CMO clients paying him five figures a month each, with a pipeline of additional prospects eager to hire him.

The unique angle Wyatt has is powerful. By becoming a Fractional CMO, he could work his way into his agency's dream clients and produce a robust marketing strategy. When it comes time for that strategy to get executed, Wyatt is able to get a proposal from his own agency and consider if they're the right team for the job or not.

This is both ethical and incredibly supportive for his client. By serving as an organization's Fractional CMO, Wyatt is able to find more work for his agency; work that he would have never found before through the high-level strategy calls his agency previously provided. This turns into better results for his clients, deeper and longer relationships, and more ease in the agency. As you know, a long-term client that pays on time, is a joy to work with, and experiences dramatic growth is the perfect type of client to have.

Another reason Wyatt joined the CMOx Accelerator was his desire to have a peer group of like-minded marketers. The trouble with owning an agency is that everyone that works for you is your subordinate and they simply don't understand the lifestyle of the business owner. Once Wyatt joined the CMOx Accelerator, he quickly found his people. He could bounce ideas and tactics off other experienced marketers, share his favorite new tools and learn what was happening in marketing across different markets.

Watch Wyatt share his thoughts and experience on becoming a Fractional CMO in his video at CMOx.co/grow

CHAPTER 2

Should You Become a Fractional CMO?

A t 7:50 a.m. on a Friday in the fall of 2015, my then girlfriend, now wife Adelaide, and I walked into a small conference room on the Hamburger University campus, a training center at the global headquarters of McDonald's Corporation in Chicago, Illinois. But we weren't there for a degree in Hamburgerology.

The smell of sandalwood drifted through the room, billowing from a pair of essential oil diffusers.

We had flown in from New Orleans and were in the company of twenty-some strangers.

Our lives were about to change, and we hardly knew it.

Over the next few days, we were going to do *the work*.

As a marketer, I had the opportunity of supporting a personal development project called Lifebook. The project was masterminded by a couple in the Chicagoland area after they had seen significant success in envisioning their future and making it come true.

They had created their own vision boards for twelve different areas of their lives: health and fitness, intellectual life, career, love relationship, quality of life, parenting, and more.

After the cajoling of friends, they decided to formalize their process and teach it to others.

> The magic of being a marketer is in surrounding yourself with incredibly talented inventors, thinkers, and doers.

The event we attended was a bootcamp to give us the time and focus to plan our lives. It was the opportunity to make a real plan—one that included our vision and the strategy we were going to follow to achieve our dreams.

Some people call this type of practice "manifesting." Others think of it as vision building or dream mapping.

No matter the name, the effect is the same: when we give ourselves the time and space to consider our lives, our quality of life, our impact and our vision for ourselves, incredible things can happen.

Before we go any further in discussing the opportunity of being a Fractional CMO, I first want to spend a few minutes with you thinking about yourself, your life and what you're going to do with the little time you have on this pale blue dot.

If nothing else, I want you to use this book as an opportunity to check in with yourself and reflect. Then I'll ask you to choose your own adventure. If that adventure aligns with the rest of the book, you'll enjoy the next few chapters on what's possible and how to become a successful Fractional CMO. If not, we can part ways and you can do the thing you were meant to do.

What Are You Solving For?

> Grab the worksheet here: CMOx.co/toolkit

The first question you must ask yourself as you consider a role or career change is:

What are you solving for?

You took the time to purchase this book and you've read this far. There must be something you want.

What is it?

Do you want to make more money?

Do you want to make a bigger impact on the world?

Do you want to tap back into the passion you first had when you started in marketing?

Do you want to have complete control over your time? Maybe live in an RV and travel the continent for a few years?

Do you want freedom?

Whatever it is that you want, write it down on the worksheet.

Example:

I am solving for: maximize time with my family, impact, and income

Next, write down where you are right now. Write things that are measurable. Something that can be recorded with a video camera or taken a photo of, such as your income, the time you spend on work, and the activities that characterize your life.

If you own an agency or get paid and have a lot of delivery costs, just put down what you're taking home. As they say, revenue is vanity, profit is sanity.

Example:

Right now I am:

- Working 60 hours a week
- Making $5,000 a month
- Not taking vacations

One Year from Today

Now I want you to think about where you want to be in one year from today. I like a 1-year timeframe because it's far away, but not too far away. If you focused on your health, your marriage, your spirituality, your career *intently* for one year, you could absolutely go to the next level.

Write down three measurable outcomes that you want to achieve in one year.

Example:

In one year, I will:

- Work 25 hours a week
- Make $25,000 a month
- Take quarterly vacations

Include things like religious donations, volunteering, writing that book you've always wanted, taking the entire month of December off… whatever you want.

Want to make a bunch of money and not work at all? Try marrying into wealth, I guess?

Anchor yourself in reality *and* believe in yourself. I bet you're one of those "overnight successes" that just needs a good couple of months of focus to break into the next level.

Get Energy, Give Value

In the next section, I want you to define two things:

1. Energy – What work do you do that gives you the most energy?
2. Value – What work do you do that provides your clients with the most value?

See if you can identify the intersection of these two categories: where your client gets maximum value and you get maximum enjoyment.

Spending as much time as possible doing this type of work will give you a lifetime of interest, and if you stay focused, it can be the foundation for your future.

Example:

> The cross section of what provides me energy and gives my clients maximum value is:
>
> * Marketing strategy
> * Finding the "big idea"
> * Supporting the team in the execution

Maybe you're more of a data wonk and you love KPIs. Or you're creative and love leading creative strategy, branding and positioning.

If you're anything like me, you enjoy *doing* the marketing work but not nearly as much as coming up with the marketing strategy.

You may even love thinking through marketing strategy all the time, giving ideas out to friends, rethinking marketing campaigns you see online or in print.

Last, if you want to spend more time on Energy and Value, you're going to have to take some things off your plate. This is where delegation comes in.

Delegate to Win

What are three things you can delegate? If you're honest with yourself, you can likely find someone else to do these tasks who are *better* at them than you. With a worldwide workforce, it's fleetingly improbable that you're the best person for these delegation tasks.

Example:

Three tasks I can delegate off my plate forever:

- Media buying
- KPI collection and reporting
- All tech, copywriting, design

On the list of my worst skills, singing and design are neck-and-neck at the top. While I can muster a semi-decent design if I must, it comes with frustration and a little anxiety, and often robs me of my confidence. Yuck!

Have you been doing copywriting and funnel building for clients, on top of marketing strategy? I wager a bet that you can have someone else take your marketing strategy direction and produce 90% or better than what you could do.

Now the rubber meets the road.

Effective Hourly Rate

You work a certain number of hours a week, on average. You also bring home a certain amount every month. Using this information, let's calculate your Effective Hourly Rate to help you understand the impact you're making and how a little shift in what you do can dramatically increase the value your clients receive. This means you can work less, or make *a lot* more, or both. It's really up to you.

When new members join the CMOx Accelerator, I have them calculate their Effective Hourly Rate (EHR). In nearly all of these calls, the member is aghast at how low their EHR is.

Here's how to calculate your EHR:

If you're working 60 hours a week and bringing home $5,000 a month in profit (pre-tax), you're making about $20.80 an hour.

Example:

> $5,000 a month
> Working 60 hours a week
> Assuming 4 weeks a month
>   = $20.80 EHR

X®

The point of EHR is to better your best, not to measure yourself against anyone else. Stay in your lane and stay focused.

It doesn't matter what you make; there's no morality in your income. Although having a higher EHR gives you the means to do things those with a lower EHR cannot do. Bringing home a couple of thousand dollars a month while living in a low-cost-of-living city or country, committing yourself to taking care of an ailing family member or spending time living out your passions in art or music—all of these life choices are all valid. It's also cool if you get your kicks working with big companies and making a lot of money.

Next, define what your EHR must be for the 1-year future you envisioned for yourself.

Example:

> $25,000 a month
> Working 25 hours a week
> Assuming 4 weeks a month
> = $250 EHR

You now know your current Effective Hourly Rate and your Target Effective Hourly Rate.

If you're caught up in thinking that you can never charge your Target Effective Hourly Rate, I wonder if you already are? Just consider the tasks you do every week. There are high-value tasks and low-value tasks, as described below. If you only did your high-value tasks and removed the low-value tasks off your plate, would your Effective Hourly Rate be at or near your Target Effective Hourly Rate?

Let me show you what I mean…

Odds are, when you work, you do work that you can bucket into four categories:

$ Tasks – These are the lowest-value tasks you perform. You may be able to hire someone in a low-cost-of-living country for less than $10 an hour to do these tasks. Things like searching for information, finding tech tools, making basic website updates, etc. In many cases, these types of tasks can be fully automated through software including middleware like Zapier.

$$ Tasks – I think of these as $10–50/hour tasks. They are the life-blood of most agencies. From website design to building out a Google Ads campaign, this work is valuable though nearly always delegatable.

$$$ Tasks – Now things are getting interesting. These tasks include leading a team meeting, breaking up a big project into smaller tasks, and a lot of the day-to-day marketing strategy. If you can spend most of your time here, you'll be rewarded for providing more value for your clients.

$$$$ Tasks – Go-to-market strategies, quarterly marketing plans and big ideas that can forever change the trajectory of a company; these tasks are fewer in quantity but the impact is asymmetric to the time spent on them.

Throughout your typical month of work, you likely do a mix of these four buckets.

If you could just stop doing the $ and $$ tasks and focus your time on the $$$ and $$$$ tasks, your impact would be dramatic.

Spending one hour doing a $ task is not worth the same to your clients as doing one hour of $$$ or $$$$ tasks, right?

What's the Difference in the Quality of Problems You're Solving Now versus What You Must Solve in One Year?

The mantra I want you to embody moving forward is to:

When you commit to solving bigger problems, you will find that the following happens:

1. You create a vacuum below you that you're forced to fill. Tasks that you used to spend long hours and low leverage on will be left undone unless you can replace yourself. Delegation is the key to this (see the upcoming chapter on delegation!).
2. You put yourself in the way of big problems. They start coming to you. In actuality, they've always been in front of you, but you've been too busy working on small problems to notice.
3. Once you solve big problems, you start to see the fun and impact. It becomes addicting. You want to do more and more. The meta-level problem solving becomes a mental exercise instead of a game of whack-a-mole with the small problem du jour.
4. You become known, talked about, revered and desired. This is the cycle of: getting better → making an impact → experiencing joy and confidence → becoming known as the person who can solve these types of problems → having bigger and better problems come to you.

It's thrilling.

What Role Can Satisfy $250+ Per-Hour and Offer 25 to 40 Hours/Week of Work?

It's no surprise that the answer is: The role of the Fractional CMO.

In my opinion, $250 an hour is the bottom end of the Effective Hourly Rate a Fractional CMO must charge. Higher rates are absolutely possible, and with a little optimization and opportunity with certain types of clients, it's possible for this EHR to be much *much* higher. Check the chapter on asymmetric upside to learn more.

Do you want to be the decision-maker when it comes to the problems that you solve, the impact that you make, the money that you bring home? Are you prepared to solve for the freedom and lifestyle that you want? Is the Fractional CMO role for you?

Perhaps becoming a Fractional CMO is right for you.

Before we get clear on what exactly it means to do the work of a Fractional CMO, check out Shannon's story on how she transformed into a Fractional CMO and tripled her income in two months...

Shannon Murray-Doffo Added $28,500 in Monthly Recurring Revenue as a Fractional CMO from 2 Sales in 2 Months!

First of all, Shannon is a different breed. She's someone who already had a ton of marketing leadership experience and a deep network well before she joined the CMOx Accelerator.

Shannon led marketing campaigns in North America for AWS and spent 15 years working for tech in cybersecurity and distribution.

Ultimately, corporate life wasn't for her. She wanted to spend more time with her partner and her son. When I asked her about including her in the book, she said:

"I am all in favor of helping the Great Resignation know that there are more humane ways to live your life than as a full-time employee."

When she joined, she was already serving a single client as their Fractional CMO. In her onboarding call with me, she said that her 90-day goal was to add $15,000 a month in recurring business. 57 days later, she smashed her target by winning two clients both north of $13,000 a month.

Here's what she said when I asked her what value she found in the Accelerator:

"I think what has helped me most is the ability to deliver excellence for my clients and having a system that I can follow that brings me the confidence I've been looking for. I'm also charging clients what I'm worth now."

If you're transitioning out of a full-time employee role and want to become a Fractional CMO, know that you're in great company.

CHAPTER 3

What Is a Fractional CMO?

It might sound like a complicated concept, but being a Fractional CMO is pretty straightforward.

What is a Fractional CMO?

Simple.

A Fractional CMO is a CMO.

They sit at the executive table but are not bound by the same limitations as a full-time employee. As a result, they are able to work for multiple businesses, offering just a fraction of their time to each organization.

Some organizations may be hesitant to hire fractional CMOs, thinking a fractional CMO cannot offer the same value as a full-time CMO. However, the reality is entirely the opposite. Process-driven Fractional CMOs provide their companies with as much attention as they need to grow and achieve their goals. The money saved between hiring full-time and fractional can then be deployed on technical marketing talent or ad spend.

Leadership as a Fractional CMO

Taking on the role of a fractional CMO will require you to change the way you operate as a marketer.

One of the biggest shifts you must make is to change your perspective…

From "I have to do this" to "this has to get done."

The reasoning behind this is simple—a Fractional CMO can't do everything. You can't be an expert of every tool and strategy in marketing. Your job is to set the marketing strategy, lead your department, and ensure that the company's growth targets are achieved.

That means you need to create a robust marketing strategy, identify the necessary campaigns, build a team, and launch the campaigns according to your plan.

Note that building a team is an integral part of this process. Rather than doing all the work on your own, you must delegate to your team or agencies. When you're surrounded by a smart, hardworking, "we'll google it before we ask you, boss!" team, your ability to execute complex marketing campaigns skyrockets.

Some people think that delegating duties is inefficient since you have to teach other people skills that you already have. It may feel like you're wasting time training other people because you could handle the work by yourself, anyway.

But you need to move away from this growth-limiting mentality.

Doing everything by yourself prevents your team members from growing and getting better at their jobs. By not delegating duties, you are taking away their opportunities for critical thinking and barring them from bringing creative ideas to the table.

I'm regularly impressed with the creative ideas my team members share.

Micromanagement curbs innovation. It also pisses team members off.

When you manage a team as their CMO, you must push people to deliver on outcomes and not just play the "stay busy" game.

For example, say you're launching a webinar. A wide range of activities need to be performed to ensure a successful launch:

- Who's in charge of the content?
- What's the hook?
- What's the call to action?
- Who is the target audience?
- Who'll take care of the slide design?
- What technology will you use? Will you stick to Zoom or try other platforms?
- How should you promote the webinar? Is there a person who can drive cold traffic? Are you going to email your list?
- How will results be tracked and attributed across platforms?

You might be confident in your ability to perform all these tasks, but that's not the job you're hired for. Your role is to determine the potential problems of launching the webinar and to resolve them from a high level.

That's why you need to assign each team member a particular duty and make sure they deliver on the necessary outcomes.

This lets you stay elevated and focused on **solving bigger problems**. This includes rallying the team around a shared outcome and ensuring everyone is on the same page.

You just have to make sure that you're working at the executive level and not as a rank-and-file employee. Again, your job is to find high-level solutions to big problems. That means tasks like setting up technology, building websites, and any other part of *executing* your strategies should be delegated.

Example:

Typical micromanagement conversation to a direct report:

"I need you to change this headline to say… then I want the font color changed to… and then make me a 1200x1200 graphic to use on the webinar platform… Once that's done, come back and I'll give you the next set of tasks."

The elevated CMO conversation to a direct report:

> "For the slides, follow the design guide. If you notice anything missing in the design guide, please propose the additions you'd like to have. We also need all graphics for the webinar. Please deliver them by Thursday at noon. Cool?"

The difference here is assigning an outcome instead of a task.

If your direct report doesn't know how to achieve the outcome but is permitted a budget to learn and time to research, you'll be able to step back and watch them achieve the target without much intervention.

It's really a beautiful thing. I've heard direct reports say things like "Thank you for trusting me on this. At the start, I was clueless, but I'm really proud of this and want to keep working on it."

Can you imagine the impact you're able to make in the lives of your direct reports? Incredible.

In a later chapter, we'll be discussing the role of the Marketing Technician and ensuring you're never left having to do the marketing labor yourself. This is a required role if you're going to work with any client; they must either have someone in the Marketing Technician seat or the budget to hire. Otherwise, you'll end up doing the marketing labor yourself.

If your client doesn't have enough money to hire someone to do the work, they might not be the right client for you. Their revenue, profit, or budget may be too small and either you need to wait a year or two for them to grow large enough or redirect them to a marketing agency that may be able to "do it all."

An issue you may run into when prospecting for clients is finding eager, fast-moving startups who want to bring you on board.

Sometimes it's the perfect match.

Other times, the startup is too small and underfunded. Over time, they ask you for more and more without increasing your pay, desperate for any additional help they can get.

I'm not suggesting you rule out startups. Just be cautious of any company without the revenue to cover your fee for six months or more at a time.

You want to work with an organization that lets you grow and earn what you should be earning as their CMO.

This means your personal sales pipeline needs to include a variety of great clients, so you never have to sell yourself short by working with clients who cannot afford your services at full rate.

I learned this lesson a long time ago: **Charge full price, or give it away for free.** There's no middle ground. No discounts. This will simplify your sales process and help you be honest with yourself about any potential opportunity.

Still, this doesn't mean you won't face challenges while working with big companies with luscious, beautiful budgets. They can still be slow to hire, slow to approve expenses, or have leadership that sucks the life out of everyone they come in contact with.

On rare occasions, you may find yourself in a pickle with a client. There may be an urgent request for the department and your team lacks the ability to do the thing. For example, you may have to set up a vanity domain redirect in a short period of time. In these rare instances, you may want to step in and do the work yourself. This is how leaders lead: we show by example and when the need arises, we may charge into battle ourselves.

Seldom are these occasions actually as urgent as they seem. If you can take space and delegate the responsibility to another person, you'll be able to stay elevated and see the next problem to solve.

Then again, sometimes a little tactical work is fun. I've been known to write a sales email or ad copy and give it to the team because the espresso hit just right and I felt called to do it. Just don't make a habit of it.

This is the shift in getting things done without doing it yourself.

Why Fractional CMOs Are the Future of Digital Marketing

When I took my first steps in the marketing industry, my goal wasn't to become a Fractional CMO.

I just wanted to make the most money on an hourly basis while providing marketing solutions and strategies to help exceptional companies scale.

Ascending to the top role in marketing was the logical next step. In doing so, I didn't have to become an expert on fast-changing subjects such as the intricacies of SEO or knowing what PPC networks have the best CPM.

And lucky I did, because it has become abundantly clear that Fractional CMOs are the future of digital marketing.

But why is that?

It's because working as a Fractional CMO offers nearly unlimited freedom for yourself while granting clients the same privileges as having a full-time CMO at a discounted rate. Moreover, the *range* you have in experience throughout your career only grows as you serve multiple clients. If you consider yourself a generalist or a Jill-of-all-trades, the Fractional CMO role will only widen your range while deepening your abilities as a leader.

Everyone in the company recognizes you as their CMO. Yet you don't have to spend 50–60 hours a week in one organization. In fact, you'll work for multiple companies, focusing on the most important duties while delegating the rest to their full-time employees, contractors, consultants and agencies.

Lawyers were one of the first disciplines to take on this "fractional" model by selling high-value services on an hourly or contract basis. CFOs followed and have done a great job serving companies as fractional CFOs. Fractional CMOs are the next logical evolution in the fractional c-suite.

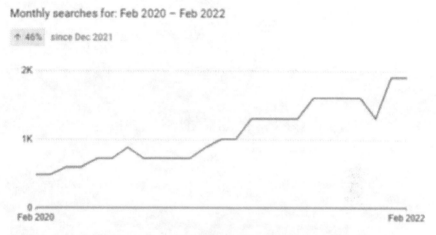

150% increase in "Fractional CMO" searches as reported by Google Ads Keyword Planner since the start of the COVID-19 pandemic

In March 2020, as COVID-19 took hold of the global economy, many didn't think the impact would be long-lasting. Years later, the death grip has started to subside and markets are slowly rebounding. All along, many of these companies experienced incredibly low revenue, and in many cases, lost money.

Every SEO firm I knew at the time had lost 90% of their business within the first week of COVID lockdowns.

Website builds, app development, conferences all ceased.

But the one role in marketing that *expanded?* You already know the answer.

And it makes sense, right? During lockdowns, there was near-zero foot traffic in businesses. Any business that relied on in-person sales realized pretty quickly that they had to sell online. Furthermore, as nearly the entire workforce was forced to work from home, companies started to see the possibilities of a fully remote team.

These companies needed a marketing strategy. They needed the strategy deployed. They needed a marketing leader. But their budget couldn't cover the full-time headcount required.

As a Fractional CMO, I didn't lose *any* business. In part, I was lucky because my clients were able to focus on digital sales. Also, I offered the ticket for them *out* of the economic trainwreck they were headed towards.

When the market is down, it's critical for businesses to keep marketing.

When the market is up, it's still critical for businesses to keep marketing.

If you sell a marketing strategy and get that strategy deployed, you become the meal ticket everyone needs.

As an exercise, sit and think for yourself: What must the market conditions be for the role of the Fractional CMO to decline? There are over 30 million small and medium-sized businesses (SMBs). It would take a black swan event to change where this ship is heading.

The freedom as a Fractional CMO is unique, too. Once your pipeline is full and you're confident in your ability to sell, you become the shot caller of your life.

Don't like a client? Frustrated that you have to be on video every day for a client call? You can let them go and bring in a new client. Think of it as *replacement therapy.*

On average, it takes 17 years or so for a marketer to become CMO. But you can pick up a single client as a Fractional CMO very quickly and go claim the title without waiting. Many of our members in the CMOx Accelerator have won their first client in 30 or 45 days, earning $10,000 a month or more per client.

It's kind of crazy to think that you're just a sale away from an extra $120,000 a year in income. Think about what one new sale a quarter would do for your confidence and your family?

The Good and Bad News of the CMO Role

The executive search firm Spencer Stuart reported in their 2021 *CMO Tenure Study* that the average CMO held their post for just 25.5 months, a significant decline from the 30-month tenure seen in 2019.

Yikes!

The CMO role is the shortest-lived executive role in today's market. That's because CMOs tend to get cycled out if certain outcomes are not achieved. It's like a sports team replacing a coach if the year didn't go as planned. Or worse, I've seen CMOs hit their targets, only to lose their job due to their company being acquired.

On the other side of the coin, there is good news particularly for women. Female CMOs now make up over 47% of CMO positions as of 2020, a dramatic increase from a 1:2 ratio in 2018.

What should you do with this data?

If you're committed to becoming the top role in marketing, the CMO, you ought to not have just one client. It's too dangerous. Once you're hired, the clock starts ticking. 2 years is not very long. Even if you absolutely crush it for your client, every month beyond a 2-year term feels like a gift. It would be much better to enjoy the pay of a CMO but have the foundation and safety of having multiple clients.

The Fractional CMO Mindset

I've mentioned several shifts you need to make to succeed as a Fractional CMO. Besides delegating duties and shedding bad clients, you also need to get into the Fractional CMO mindset.

One component of the required mindset is to distinguish between **new and different tasks versus routine tasks**—and filling your team members' plates according to their capacity.

Let me explain.

Each member of your team has a different skill set. Some may be highly effective at solving unfamiliar challenges. You assign it, they jump on it and take care of it. But afterwards, they'd be rearing to take on a new challenge, which means you can't keep assigning them to the same things. Their skill set is better suited for novelties, so try not to overwhelm them with routine tasks.

On the other hand, some people thrive when it comes to routine tasks. They can perform the same tasks week after week, and they get better and better every time they do it. This means they are better suited for repetitive or recurring tasks. You need both of these conations across your direct reports.

As a leader, you need to accommodate their preferences with the right task type. This gives you a reliable team that continues to get energy and excitement from their work and professional growth. You ought to consider conation while interviewing potential candidates for your client, or when you start working with a client and you meet their team.

For example, you might be looking for someone to fill a role where they would eventually have to take on routine tasks. To find the right person, you need to carefully analyze the skills and personality of those applying for the role to determine if they're up to par.

If a candidate describes their work style as consistent or something similar, and they fit in well with the company's culture and core values, you'll know you've found the right person for the job.

The reason is simple—routine work requires consistency.

On the other hand, a role that requires taking on new, unfamiliar outcomes that lack structure should be filled by someone who enjoys fast-changing environments.

Again, this is something you have to nail right from the interview stage.

But once you think you've got the right people in all the right seats, your job doesn't end there.

Having the fractional CMO mindset means always being on top of task delegation and making sure the people you hire are actually performing roles the company needs, getting the necessary outcomes met, and that they're the right culture fit.

This mindset doesn't stop once you've made a hire.

You should regularly analyze the task delegation in your companies and make appropriate adjustments based on the natural behavior of the individuals.

What are your routine tasks, and who's in charge of them? Are the people responsible good at them, or do they keep failing? How about your new, unfamiliar tasks? Are the people tasked to work on them creative enough to solve new problems?

If not, you should consider re-assigning these tasks to different team members. Just make sure their skill sets match the requirements for each role. Team satisfaction will rise, more will get done, and you'll be seen as the leader the company needs.

Create an Ever-Increasing Future

Picture yourself at a crossroads, where you'll have to choose one path over the other.

The first path promises a standard direction that will bring you to a standard future. A typical 9–5 job, a consistent paycheck that only increases marginally every year, and a standard corporate ladder to climb.

Then, there's the second path. One that has no standard directions, but one where you can pave your own way to an incredible, ever-expanding future.

Which one will you take?

Personally, I've been at this crossroads many times in my life.

I always chose the second path—the path that led to me becoming a Fractional CMO.

Now, why is that?

Well, Dan Sullivan, one of my mentors, has an iconic line that has always stuck with me:

"Always make your future bigger than your past."

I could have mowed lawns forever.

I could have been an adjunct marketing professor to this day.

I could have worked in a marketing agency well into my retirement years.

But I didn't want to take the standard path.

Many people do.

In fact, you may have gone to school with a valedictorian, homecoming king, or an all-star football quarterback. Naturally, this person was very popular and attractive—back then. But the moment they decide to take the standard path, it leads them to the end of the road.

So, during class reunions and random run-ins, all they could talk about are their scholastic achievements—how successful and popular they were in their college days. They are stuck in a glorious past, because the future just doesn't hold much for them.

But I didn't want my biggest achievements to be the ones I collected back in school.

I preferred the path where I could create ever-expanding opportunities for my future self.

This is exactly why I chose to become a fractional CMO, rather than a full-time one. Because becoming a full-time CMO is not much different from the various paths I've tried earlier in my career.

It would have bound me to the office for 60-hour weeks where I could only take home a minute percentage of the wealth I created for other people. Worse, it would have taken a toll on my marriage and other aspects of my personal life.

After my business fell apart and I lost nearly all my revenue, I reflected a lot on my career choice. After running the numbers and thinking through my future a hundred times, I finally committed to myself that I would be a Fractional CMO and do whatever it took to be successful. Since my days in Boy Scouts, I have carried a pocket knife. That winter, I had my Benchmade knife engraved with the word "inevitable" to remind myself that my success and growth is inevitable as long as I keep betting on myself.

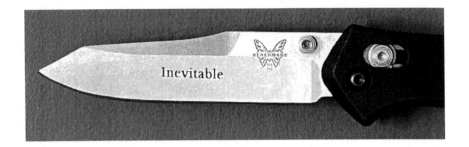

Taking on a full-time CMO role would have been the end of the road for my "inevitable" mantra.

But by choosing the path of being a Fractional CMO…

I took control of my own time, working only with clients and individuals I love working with.

I delegated the tasks to my direct reports, getting paid for strategizing, leading and bringing in top solutions for clients. The clients I've worked with have changed me. I've gotten to witness great leadership and terrible leadership by CEOs. I get to see what different company types look like from the inside. I am better by leaps and bounds year over year. The quality of people I am surrounded with grows every year, as do the opportunities I'm presented with.

What other role exists where you can grow this quickly, get presented with opportunities to impact swaths of people, get well compensated and have control over your time? Not many.

Master Slow-to-Change Principles

If you've been in marketing for more than a few years, you've seen some major changes in the landscape. You might remember the website Ezine Articles and how Google's algorithm update *slapped* this and similar article sites that were producing a high volume of low-quality content back in 2011. In a moment, article sites like Ezine Articles were actively penalized.

Or maybe you remember the old trick of keyword stuffing in the footer of a website. The idea was to write as many permutations of a keyword as possible, then hide the ugly block of text in a background that matched the font color.

There was a high time for ad arbitrage, too, where savvy marketers would drive cheap Taboola traffic to a landing page that had a dozen links. These marketers would spend $0.05 for the click and receive $0.08 or more for the prospect clicking on an ad on their page.

Then there were the ever-changing white hat techniques in SEO, where marketers would study every word from Google SEO expert Matt Cutts.

Incredible techniques were found and leveraged to help grow companies.

But they were all short-lived.

The marketers that followed these fast-to-change techniques would strike gold for a few days or months, amass all the wins they could, then watch in horror as their meal ticket disappeared due to an algorithm update or shift in policy.

The slow-and-steady winners year after year were those who committed themselves to the slow-to-change principles of marketing.

Slow-to-change principles of marketing include:

- How to write a great offer
- How to build rapport with a prospect
- Tracking and building data insights on customer behavior

The tools and platforms may change every month, but the principles live on forever.

If you are going to build your business as a marketer, I suggest you learn slow-to-change principles that you can master year over year for your clients. You'll find your stress is much lower and your ability to produce predictable results is much greater than if you were to focus on rapidly changing tactic-based marketing "tricks."

When you're ready to deploy a campaign, you can always hire an expert in that field who is abreast of the fast-changing techniques. Let them run rabid, searching for the next *hack* while you master identifying the problem, building the team, and getting the results needed through effective delegation.

Showcase Your A-Game

Many marketing executives think there's no alternative to being a full-time CMO. They enjoy the politicking and ladder climbing of traditional corporate life.

But as you've seen in this chapter, full-time CMOs aren't the way of the future. Fractional CMOs are taking the world by storm.

On one hand, you enjoy nearly unlimited freedom in choosing how to render your services. You can determine how much time you dedicate to each client. Best of all, you can easily surpass the earnings of full-time CMOs (and work less) by working with select clients.

On the other hand, fractional CMOs are becoming increasingly popular since they're more affordable. They're especially useful for companies who need a sound marketing strategy and a leader who can steer them in the right direction, but who don't need it 40 hours a week.

However, taking on the road less traveled and succeeding in this industry doesn't come without a significant commitment on your part. Just to recap, the first thing you need to do is follow the right mindset. Acknowledge there's a range of tasks in your business (new and different versus routine) and delegate them according to your team's conation.

And again, you might want to jump in and handle all the work, but this goes against why you became a Fractional CMO. Instead, trust your team to carry out their duties effectively, and you'll be able to focus on crucial leadership aspects.

All these tactics will put you on the right track to creating an ever-increasing future. You'll no longer be limited to having a standard future—and all your efforts will be geared towards future prosperity.

The first thing you need to be a Fractional CMO is to have red-hot leads who want to hire you. We'll cover that in the next chapter.

CHAPTER 4

Red-Hot Leads

In December of 2013, I was the lead marketer on an interesting project: to help Jordan Belfort promote his "Straight Line Persuasion" course on the backside of his Scorsese-directed *The Wolf of Wall Street* movie release.

The stakes were incredibly high and the market was already overwhelmed with the winter holiday promotion madness that starts every November and lasts until December 25th.

Still, we had a job to do: to produce a world-class launch and sell millions of dollars of Jordan's course. It was no easy task. The fast-paced iterations, the website rebuild, the follow-up email sequences for all the different types of leads, and generating an all-time record in sales.

In 2013, technology was different than it is today. Facebook didn't have a pixel to track conversions the way it does now. In many ways, we were blind, even without UTMs due to cross-domain tracking issues.

Despite the difficult environment, the promotion was a smashing success. We sold millions of dollars of courses and built a mailing list of over 100,000 leads.

One of the biggest lessons I learned from the promotion was the difference in lead quality and the importance of qualified and eager leads.

During our brainstorming sessions, we realized that there would be three types of leads that would visit Jordan's website:

1. People who loved the movie
2. People who loved Jordan's story
3. People who wanted to be successful like Jordan

All the DiCaprio fans fell into the first bucket. Then there were the leads who enjoyed Jordan's story, especially the quaaludes scene. They would never become a customer of Jordan's courses or purchase tickets to his events.

The final bucket is where the money was: relevant, interested, and hot leads.

When we emailed the third bucket, open rates were through the roof.

But over time, they declined rapidly.

The half-life on email open rates was 2–3 weeks. Our 60% open rate soon dropped to 30%, then to 15%, then to sub-10%.

Hot leads cool off.

The same is true in your business as a Fractional CMO.

You've got to know your ideal client: there may be plenty of people who want to talk to you, but are they interested and able to buy what you're selling?

Then build authority: people need to know why *you* are the right person for them.

Then fill your funnel: a funnel of qualified, hot leads is your ticket to anything you want in business.

Finally, you must keep your leads warm: cold leads don't buy.

I've seen plenty of marketers enjoy a short bout as a successful fractional CMO. The reason for the short-term success is they all had a common problem...

They would start as a mid-to-top level marketer in an organization before deciding to leave full-time employment. On their way out, they'd win some business with past clients or through a referral, which gave them an excellent starting point.

The initial success in those cases was great. People were able to transition from a full-time job to being a Fractional CMO and had every right to feel proud. They would make more than their full-time job, work less and feel as though they had made it.

But the issue I'm talking about was enough to undermine that achievement.

In most cases, the CMOs in question had six-month or 90-day contracts in their hands. As the renewal approached, the CMO would rush to create a new proposal for the next term. More often than not, those contracts ended sooner than initially predicted.

Once the contracts ended, the CMOs could only look around and realize that they didn't have the referrals, pipeline, or repeatability they needed to move forward.

Fearing they'd have skinny children, the CMOs got worried.

This is a scary situation for every aspiring Fractional CMO. You don't want to be on edge, thinking about how you could wake up one day, lose a client, and be left out on the curb. If you are the sole breadwinner in your family, the consequences of you not having a full pipeline could be devastating.

If you want to avoid that situation, you'll need a pipeline full of qualified leads. Then, you'll be able to pick up a new client whenever you need to, and that will gain you the security that you need in your business.

Without a pipeline, you might end up like I did.

When I was starting out, I also didn't have a pipeline set up. As a result, my business went from $23,000 a month to zero, and it happened almost overnight. It was as if I had started my business over from scratch.

As a Fractional CMO, you need a way to get leads systematically every week or month. Hanging your shingle as a fractional CMO without that system might have serious consequences.

In the best-case scenario, you'll still be able to win clients quickly, even without a functional pipeline. However, that will cause a lot of late-night work, stress, and frustration.

In the worst-case scenario, finding prospects will take too long. Then, your situation can quickly become dire.

You could find yourself living on credit cards or even losing your job and being unable to make the rent.

Maybe you don't think it's possible that you could lose business quickly and be without clients in the blink of an eye. Are you willing to make that bet? After all, once you go solo, there'll be no safety net for your business apart from the one you create.

Being a Fractional CMO who works outside of the comfort of a traditional full-time employee role means you have more responsibilities on your hands. You can't simply show up for work, do a good job, and expect to get paid regularly.

Instead, you'll need to be in control of your pipeline and how new clients come into your business.

Additionally, you'll need to realize that being a Fractional CMO isn't a hobby. Getting a single client who you're charging $3,000 or even $15,000 monthly will be exciting, but it won't be enough to sustain your business long-term.

If you want to take your job seriously, become renowned, and have the necessary confidence in your business, you'll need to build a pipeline.

Perhaps more importantly, your pipeline will allow you to choose your clients. And working with only the best-fit clients will be a sure way to continual, sustainable success and growth.

Envision Your Perfect Client

Years ago, when I was working in a marketing agency, we had a particular approach to work: whatever your problem was, we could solve it.

The team was always willing to do new things, be creative, and stay on the cutting edge of tech and marketing. It was a hardworking, intelligent team that took on many fun and innovative projects.

We could be everything for everybody, and that was our main issue.

You see, as entrepreneurs, consultants, or agency owners, we're conditioned to take on any business that comes our way. We chase every opportunity to exchange our services for money.

Paradoxically, this approach actually makes it difficult to make money.

When you're always doing different things for different types of clients, having any repeatability or leverage becomes nigh impossible.

Every problem you take on is new and tough, and it takes plenty of energy to solve. As a Fractional CMO, you can't afford to work that way.

You want to have repeatable results. And to achieve that, you'll need to choose clients with whom you can win.

Of course, this matter comes down to niching. You should work within a niche that allows you to place every client in a similar context. If you want to work less and earn more, it's crucial to streamline your clients.

For example, you might be able to serve a B2B SaaS, a high-volume e-commerce, and a financial service firm all at once. However, switching between those contexts will come at a substantial cost.

You could serve those clients with success but end up robbed of your free time or profits.

If you want to avoid such complications, you can use a simple guide to give you a clear picture and help you determine your perfect clients. You'll need to pay attention to four points:

- Revenue
- Team make-up
- Niche or industry
- Hacks for happiness

Looking at your client's revenue, the first thing I want to mention is that there's no wrong answer.

Your ideal clients could be startups, or they could be companies making $100 million a year. However, some nuances will be crucial moving forward.

For instance, a startup could be venture-funded, backed by family and friends, or bootstrapped. Naturally, this will affect their profile considerably. Venture capital firms will want a fast return. A bootstrapped company may want a more sustainable growth and not have access to an outsized marketing budget.

You want to work with clients who can pay you *and* whom you can help. They should be able to afford you and not risk everything in case you aren't able to deliver results. If a company has to liquidate their kids' college funds to pay you, working with them won't make sense.

Next, you'll want to look at the client's team make-up.

In many cases, when you start working with a client, they won't have a marketing department.

Of course, you don't want to be the implementer. Your role is as a strategist that can view and solve problems from an elevated position.

When looking at a prospective company, you should check if they have a capable marketing department. If they don't, see if the company has the budget to build one under your leadership. In those cases, the client's revenue will come into play once again.

Furthermore, you'll want to work with a team that you can support. Ideally, all of the people in the marketing department should continue to work there, get better, and move up in their careers. You'll want growth-oriented people to lead, though you'll be able to shuffle and possibly terminate team members once you're engaged with the client.

Again, it's simple: the client must have a marketing technician or team, or they must be willing to build one at your direction.

I've already mentioned the niche aspect. When you choose a niche, you can become well-known and seen as the leader. You can build a portfolio of companies in a niche, which makes you desirable to others in the same or adjacent niches. You'll also become an expert on the idiosyncrasies of the niche, which will reduce your time in taking a client from where they are to where they want to be.

You can use several hacks to determine whether a prospective company aligns with your goals.

One of the best hacks is very simple but extremely useful. When you have a sales call with a company, study their behavior.

Check if they're on time, listen with full attention, seem willing to commit to solving the problem, and *end the call by saying "Thank you."* If you see these signals, that might mean you have a culture-fit client on your hands.

When people are friendly and treat you with respect during sales calls, they'll likely be helpful, supportive, and dialed in to your needs. Those clients will understand that you need to be successful for their company to have success, too.

On the other end of that spectrum, you should be wary of clients who quickly pass blame around during the preliminary call. After all, as a Fractional CMO, you'll be 100% responsible for the company's marketing success. Blame cultures always backfire. You may enter the company as the hero, but that status won't last long.

Once you determine your ideal clients, you'll, naturally, need to attract them. And you'll do just that by building your authority.

Build Authority

Back when I worked at a marketing agency, a sales prospect needed us to do something we'd never done before.

The prospect was a coaching company and they needed a membership site. It was a complex job with a lot of custom integrations, but I was sure my team could handle it.

I talked to the prospect and mapped out their problems. Then, I got to work, doing my best to figure out the high-level solution from my team so I could put together a proposal. The team did a great job and we produced a new proposal that was very detailed. I was proud.

When I presented the proposal at the next call, I got feedback I wasn't expecting.

The prospect said, *"Casey, you seem like a smart guy, and there's no doubt you can figure this stuff out. But I don't want to risk my business success on people who haven't done it before."*

And they were completely right. We could have made the project work, but we would be learning along the way.

We didn't have the authority to build trust with the client.

Of course, this was mainly due to the marketing agency having the wrong approach that I mentioned earlier in this chapter. We were trying to be everything for everyone.

To build your authority, you'll have to niche down. Once you're serving a specific type of client with specific needs, you can focus on becoming better at what you do than anyone else. And the more time you spend in a particular industry, the more you'll know about it.

There are many details that you can only learn by spending enough time in a niche. You can pick up on all the shortcuts, advertising places, acceptable costs per lead, the most effective marketing campaigns, and so much more.

But you have to niche down.

Naturally, you'll choose the niche where there are clients that can pay your fees, where there's lasting and long-term growth potential, and as a bonus, where you have some experience. Then, you can start building your authority among them.

One of the crucial aspects of authority-building is desire.

You can't manufacture desire. You can't make someone want what you have. However, you can understand what your prospects want and show them how you can help them achieve that with what you offer.

Your clients will never want *you* or a Fractional CMO. They'll want the byproducts you create, whether it's revenue, freedom, ease, simplicity, scale, or anything else. In other words, they'll be interested in the endgame, and that's what you should focus on.

In that sense, you have to understand that the number one thing you're offering as a Fractional CMO is leadership.

Obviously, your job is primarily about marketing strategy and tactics. But the thing larger organizations need the most is leadership, and that's what they'll value above anything else.

Look at it this way: A mediocre strategy deployed well is worth more than a perfect strategy that's poorly deployed. You can see this all over the market. Many organizations have half-deployed marketing campaigns that aren't nearly as effective as those deployed with confidence.

That's why a perfectly curated strategy isn't the first thing your clients will require. Instead, they'll need your leadership skills to rally people around the same mission and get an outcome.

If you think back to the story about the marketing agency I used to work with, you'll notice a crucial point about building authority. That point is, you can't become an authority by only doing things you've never done before.

Instead, you should lean on areas where you have the most experience, or where a deeper experience can benefit your clients the most.

Many members of our CMOx Accelerator have chosen niches that they already know. This gave them network support and plenty of opportunities to prove their knowledge. And that's another crucial point.

If you can prove that you've done something before, you'll be more likely to win new business.

In fact, the best predictor of someone's success is that they have experience with the particular problem they're solving. And if you can provide social proof about what you've done before, you'll be on the right track.

To that end, you should produce a case study as your first step. This study needs to share who the client was and what you did for them. You'll want to cover the problem they faced, the outcome of your solution (not *how* you solved it) and a relevant data point or two. It can be a page long and contain your logo, several bullet points, and a couple of sentences.

Believe it or not, this piece of collateral will help you win more business in the beginning than anything else. No fancy website needed!

Building authority is all about proving to your prospects that you can help them and that you've done it before. A case study and some testimonials will get you a long way in that regard.

When it comes to testimonials, it's worth mentioning that video material will be the most valuable. However, if you can't produce video testimonials, written testimonials will be the next best thing.

And if, for some reason, you can't produce proper testimonials about your efficacy as a marketing leader, you can go a tier down and get people to talk about your character. Those won't be as effective as the higher tier, but they'll still give you some support.

The point is to amass social proof. The more you have, the less working with you will seem like a risk. Companies will be willing to give you a shot, and that will be your opportunity to produce results worthy of a full-blown case study.

Another form of social proof is to be featured on podcasts. This is often an easy exercise in finding the top podcasts in your niche and reaching out to the hosts, pitching them on your topic. Most potential podcast guests are shy about chasing down opportunities to speak. If you are consistent and direct, you may be surprised by how many guest spots you can get in a short period of time.

Just like an incredible product or service, if there's no marketing, nobody will know about it! You must market yourself and put yourself in front of your ideal audience in order to capture their attention and show them how you can help them achieve their outcome goals.

Fill Your Funnel

Suppose you've niched down, and you've started producing social proof to build authority. In that case, you'll know where your perfect clients are, and you'll be able to create enough trust to land some projects.

However, your work doesn't stop there.

You'll recall the issue I discussed at the beginning of this chapter. You don't want a handful of isolated projects. You need a funnel that will constantly provide new leads and clients.

To build and fill your funnel, you'll need to go through three crucial steps:

1. Get the list
2. Find a starving crowd
3. Use the golden ratio

All three steps are essential for your progress and growth, so we'll break them down in more detail here.

Get the List

Let's say you're working in a limited industry—for example, the craft beer industry. The first thing you'll want to do is identify every craft brewery in your region or in the country and figure out who the owners are.

Then, you'll get their contact information.

There are many ways to get that info. You can research online, hire someone to pull the info, or purchase databases. In any case, the critical point is to get it done. This is a basic rule in marketing: get the list!

Granted, there are certain industries where getting contacts will be more challenging. You may want to choose a niche where the list is easy to get.

You'll probably be able to find partnerships that will put you in a position where the list will be more accessible. One of our CMOx Accelerator members was able to work out a work-trade relationship with a list broker. He provided a short sprint of marketing strategy for the list broker and in exchange received the list he needed; that's a win-win.

An alternative route may be to find companies who already have a relevant list and sell a non-competitive product or service to yours and offer them a commission if they send emails on your behalf.

This way, you'll get to sell to their list, they won't lose any money, and both parties will actually profit from the deal.

The point I want to make here is really straightforward. You *have* to get the contact list of your prospects, and there's always a way to do it.

One thing is particularly worth thinking about when gathering contact information. Examine the clients you're currently working with and those you want to close. Then, try to find a definitive list of those clients somewhere online.

Whichever way you go about it, remember that getting a list of clients will be paramount for your business. Once you have the needed contacts, you can develop a strategy and process to leverage them.

The Ultimate Advantage

One of the all-time greatest copywriters and marketers, Gary Halbert, used to teach copywriting courses. During one lecture, he asked the students an intriguing question:

"If you and I both owned a hamburger stand and were competing to sell the most burgers, which advantages would you like to have to help you win?"

Students started giving various answers. They said they would want the best beef available, the freshest buns, Amish cheddar cheese, or top-quality sides and pickles.

Other students focused on the best value, lowest price, or the ability to give extra drinks and fries free of charge.

Once the students finished with the lengthy list of their desired advantages, Gary said there was only one advantage he would want: a starving crowd.

This is precisely what you want as a Fractional CMO. You want a starving crowd that will crave everything you can offer. If your clients are starving, they'll line up with bated breath.

Now, that in no way means I'm encouraging you to do anything less than great things for your clients. It simply means that a starving crowd will likely start working with you faster.

This principle easily translates into your work as a Fractional CMO. You want to create relationships with companies that really need you. If they're thinking about whether or not they'll invest in marketing at all, they're not your crowd.

Companies on the fence will be more reluctant to say yes. On the other hand, starving clients will jump at the opportunity. Companies that have a strategic plan to grow their business over the next 3–5 years will understand the need for marketing support ASAP to ensure they're on track.

But how do you fill your funnel with starving prospects?

Well, the answer is pretty straightforward if you have a list. Not all contacts on your list will fit the bill. To find the best matches, you'll need to focus on businesses that are growing quickly.

When companies are moving fast, it means they're hungry for growth. And if they're not there yet, you'll need to wait for the perfect moment to engage them.

Businesses sometimes take a while to pick up speed, and you don't want to start working with them in the middle of that process. Wait until the needs of your prospects become urgent and look for some tell-tale signs of that situation.

For example, when a company is hiring marketing staff, that might be a good moment to jump in with your offer. Or they might show interest, but something is blocking them from moving forward with you.

When you notice those signals, you have to be ready to react. At the same time, you must be willing to wait for the right moment. If a company is hiring their first marketing person, they may be too nascent to need a Fractional CMO. Their immediate goal may be to just write a couple of emails and have an active social media strategy. Right strategy or not, the organization's immaturity in marketing is typically a turn-off for the seasoned fractional CMO.

To fill your funnel with a starving crowd, look for businesses that have gone through a significant shift. Maybe they just got acquired, or they acquired another company. Perhaps they were awarded a license or received a Series A funding.

Your ideal prospects should be starving for *leadership*. That's when they'll be needing you the most.

The Golden Ratio

The golden ratio is a well-known rule used in arts, architecture, math, and many other disciplines. In business, there's a unique golden ratio that is used to describe a company that has a flywheel spinning.

The basic notion is that referrals come in more frequently than customers churn. Let me explain this principle in more detail.

As a Fractional CMO, you should have long-term engagements and relationships. You should work with clients for six months, a year, or more.

Full-time CMOs typically stick around for about two years—pretty shocking, right? The role of the full-time CMO is the shortest-lived c-suite role. As a Fractional CMO, you should aim to stay with a client for at least that long, ideally longer.

While you're working with current clients, you'll probably have referrals come in. Now, referrals come through word of mouth, which is excellent. They already come from someone who trusts you, and they're likely pre-qualified.

However, you should never build your business solely on that.

While getting a referral is excellent, the issue with it is that you stop being in control of your pipeline. In that case, your business becomes unstable and unpredictable.

On the other hand, if you have a full pipeline, you can know precisely what the next several months or even years will look like. That's why you want to base your business on your pipeline. But even that isn't the best possible solution.

The best-case scenario is to have a full pipeline *with* referrals on top of it. This brings us to the golden ratio.

If you have clients sticking around for a year or more, you'll need to get one referral every quarter.

This way, you'll have a filled-up pipeline that won't go over your capacity to serve. You'll end up with the golden ratio where referrals come in more frequently than your customers churn.

Of course, this principle opens up many new questions.

How do you plan to get referrals? How do you ask for them? How often is too often to ask?

While these questions are essential, one principle will offer a solution. You must have a pragmatic way to drive business, revenue, and new customers into your Fractional CMO practice. And that's why you shouldn't rely on referrals.

If you set up your business to function independently of referrals, you'll gain the freedom to choose how and when you bring those extra prospects in.

As I've mentioned, you should ideally bring in a referral once every quarter at a minimum.

Once you fill up your pipeline and referrals start coming in, you'll get a sense of two crucial things.

First, getting referrals is a sign that you're doing a good job. You're giving other people a reason to put their name on the line and recommend you to someone else.

Second, you get into a position of predictability. Your pipeline is full, and you're converting and serving your clients. Then, on top of that, you're getting referrals that swell your pipeline to the point where you can pick and choose between your clients, replacing those you don't like with your ideal clients.

Warm Your Leads

Imagine you did everything described in this chapter. You found your niche and identified your perfect client. You managed to build authority and a funnel filled with a starving crowd complemented by just the right number of referrals.

Everything's ready, but there's one more aspect to cover.

Now that you have your ideal prospects where you want them, you need to stay in touch with them. You have to keep your leads warm and prove your expertise over time.

How could you do that if you didn't use marketing?

One obvious answer would be to have a conversation with every individual on your list that you deem qualified.

You could hit them up and say something like, *"I see you're doing this and that. Here's what I do. Would it make sense for us to chat?"* And that could be a very effective way of reaching out.

However, you might not have the time to contact every company on your list. What then?

The first thing I'd recommend is for you to find a single communication channel to use moving forward. That may be a network like LinkedIn, Facebook, Twitter, Discord, or Slack.

But all of those networks tend to have a lot of noise going on. It may be true in your niche that the email inbox is a place reserved for communication with trusted individuals. If that's true, you may want to follow the age-old advice to email your leads at a regular cadence.

Emails will allow you to get in front of your prospects in a quiet environment that will isolate your communication from the noise.

The notion of having a single communication channel might sound counterintuitive in this day and age.

After all, so many people talk about how you need to run profiles on Instagram, Facebook, Twitter, and LinkedIn, keep them filled with content, and update them regularly. Then, on top of that, they say you should also create a podcast and branch out even further.

The issue with taking on several marketing channels is pretty simple. Every channel you add only doubles the time it will take you to reach the same level of success.

That's something people tend to forget. Keeping a profile up to date is time-consuming. I personally don't post on social media much at all. It's not required for me to be successful and it's often just a nuisance.

So why wouldn't you choose a single communication channel and win there first?

Focus on one thing and master it completely. Once you've achieved the results and gained the competence and confidence, you can move to the next channel if you desire.

If you're worried about getting started with that, you can use something I call the 30-Day Lead Nurture Sequence.

Get a copy of the 30-Day Lead Nurture Sequence at CMOx.co/toolkit

This time-tested strategy will allow you to nurture your prospects and educate them systematically. It relies on an email sequence that covers every step of the relationship between you and your clients.

The sequence will identify your client's problems, position you as the solution, create scarcity around your service, provide proof of your expertise, and, finally, give your prospects a specific call to action.

Now, I'm aware that marketers can have a particular issue about communicating with clients. It's the same problem mechanics have with their cars: we do incredible work for others, but doing it for ourselves can feel surprisingly difficult.

If this is the case for you, that's good. Feeling a bit edgy about communication might be a great edge to lean into.

Keep in mind that communication is a thing of practice. To get better and more comfortable at it, you'll simply need to talk to people more. And that's precisely what you should be doing.

The goal is to create as many conversations with your ideal clients as possible and do it regularly. Remaining front-of-mind at all times is paramount because, even if you're the perfect fit for those prospects, the time might be wrong for them right now.

Your prospects might be about to have a baby, or they just had issues in their team. They may be in the middle of hiring or pushing out a massive campaign.

In those circumstances, your ideal clients might not consider bringing you on right now, regardless of how much they need you.

The best thing you can do in such cases is to stay on their mind and keep them warm. I've had contracts signed on the same day of the initial meeting, and I've had clients who took 14 months to sign the proposal.

The differences in timing can be very dramatic, but you won't have any control over that. However, what you can control is how frequently you keep in touch with your prospects.

Here's the bumper sticker: unless they ask you to stop, keep in touch with valuable touchpoints.

A prospect that has been suitably warmed will convert much faster once you're on a call with them if you have a process to follow. Sales can feel daunting, especially if you've never sold services in the 4–5 figure a month range.

That's why the following chapter will deal with conversions and how you can make them as seamless as possible. But first, check out Jesse's story about how he transformed himself and won a big client quickly:

Agency Owner to Fractional CMO, Jesse Stoddard

For over five years, Jesse ran his own digital marketing agency. His biggest problem was one that many face every day as agency owners and marketing consultants...

Jesse found that he could sell clients into his agency, where he would provide typical agency work of website building, SEO, media buying, etc. However, the effort to identify the work was significant: In order to do a great job for his clients, Jesse couldn't give a one-size-fits-all marketing strategy and then have his team build out the campaigns.

Instead, he had to dig in deep and come up with a marketing strategy comprehensive enough to include the work he and his team could do.

The problem? He wasn't charging for the strategy.

Aside from that, his engagements were short-lived. After he provided the strategy, he and his team did the work to bring the strategy to life. Shortly thereafter, the job would be complete and the contract would be over.

These short-term contracts were a big cost to Jesse. The cost of attracting a client and converting them to a customer was not offset by long-term well-paying contracts. They were instead ~90-day contracts that left Jesse and his team hunting for the next client quickly.

If you've been in this revolving door of serving clients, you need to find a way to extend your contract length from months to years.

Jesse also had another major problem with his agency: He found himself being the "everything guy." Leading marketing strategy, writing copy, building ad campaigns, taking calls and texts after his preferred work hours... all so that he could keep his clients happy.

Lastly, Jesse lacked the accountability, coaching and community he needed to elevate himself to the next level.

Since I've gotten to know Jesse, I can see just how smart he is. He's a great marketer with a ton of experience helping clients. Given the time, he could figure out how to ascend to the role of Fractional CMO, but part of Jesse's genius is in knowing the opportunity cost of figuring it all out himself.

When he joined the CMOx Accelerator, he said, "The best athletes in the world have a coach. Why shouldn't I?"

Jesse joined on February 17 and on March 25, just five weeks and one day later, he had his first $10,000 check for his first fractional CMO client in-hand. The client had some unique requests on their terms with Jesse and I coached him on holding his ground. In the end, the client accepted Jesse's terms and paid the first month in full before Jesse even started.

Jesse regularly joins the live coaching calls and attends our quarterly planning events to build his marketing strategy and the quarterly plans for his clients. Jesse has leaned on the copywriters, media buyers, and funnel builders inside the CMOx Accelerator community to get better results for his clients in less time.

The two traits Jesse has that have made him so successful are coachability and hunger.

Coachability – Jesse knows that the best shortcut in life is finding someone who has done something before and having them coach you on the things to do. He knows that accountability and a community are what keep him focused on the effort required to build his business. The results speak for themselves.

Hunger – Jesse is hungry to grow. As soon as he won his first client, he dug in deeper on building his pipeline. Yes, $10,000 a month in new business is exciting, and it's just the beginning. With his hunger to grow, I have no doubt Jesse will become one of the top Fractional CMOs in the industry.

You can see Jesse's story in his words over at CMOx.co/toolkit

CHAPTER 5

Achieving Effortless Conversions

B eing a great marketer doesn't mean you're also an expert sales-person.

In fact, you might be the type of marketer who's a bit awkward around sales. And that's completely fine.

Some people might be born to sell, but that's by no means a prerequisite for success. With some proven methods and a bit of practice, you can move from being awkward and become completely confident in sales.

The best starting point on that journey would be to understand what sales is all about.

Sales is the process that takes people from having a need to getting a solution. In that regard, sales is the lifeblood of the world.

Our world would be nothing without entrepreneurs, since entrepreneurs make their livelihood on solving problems. But those entrepreneurs couldn't create any value without sales. Whether you have an idea, product, or expertise as a marketer, you must sell it to make an impact.

No value is created without first a sale being made.

That notion makes sales critically important and much different from the pejorative meaning people often attribute.

But selling your expertise is much more than securing a transaction. It's about how far you're willing to go to make a difference.

Here's what I mean by that.

Back in 2009, I went on a 4-month trip cycling from Madrid to Rome.

During the trip, I picked up a copy of *Never Eat Alone* where the author Keith Ferrazzi, among other things, mentioned the benefits of a 10-day silent meditation retreat. This idea resonated with me so much that I immediately got my laptop out and searched for the nearest retreat centers.

I found one in Italy, reached out, and secured my spot for a silent 10-day Vipassana meditation retreat (dhamma.org).

I spent 10 days in silence, only breaking it on the last day in community with other retreat attendees. The experience was deeply personal and forever changed my relationship to myself. Once we broke silence, I got to know one of the retreat instructors, and it turned out we had a lot in common.

His name was Greg, and he happened to be a great marketer. During our conversation, Greg asked me a question that shifted my perspective.

He asked, *"What force would you use to stop a child from touching a hot stove?"*

I think you and I are both similar: we would do *whatever* it took to stop a child from touching a hot stove, or running into traffic.

You've probably picked up how this story applies to your work as a fractional CMO and sales.

If you believe in your abilities as a marketing strategist and leader, you know you can solve massive problems for companies. You can put them out of harm's way and allow them to go out there and do good in the world.

Now, the question is, what force would you use to help those companies?

Are you going to sheepishly ask for permission to follow-up? Or are you going to stand up tall and be direct, asking important questions and challenging the prospect on their ability to grow without your help?

You can significantly impact the world and the businesses you help. But you'll have to use sales to do that.

That's the level of love sales needs. You're selling to help someone avoid suffering and solve a problem. Your prospects are that kid that's about to touch a hot stove, and you can get in front of them and help.

And the only way you can do all that is by making the sale and putting your services at the client's disposal.

Lubricate the Sale

When making a sale, you can't just jump into it. The process requires some preparation.

We call that initial stage "lubricating the sale," and it's relatively simple.

You need to produce a proposal for a prospect within 24 hours, and it has to include everything necessary to keep you safe.

This latter part means your proposal needs to cover certain aspects that will ensure your interests are represented in the project as much as the client's.

One particular thing that gets overlooked in proposals is your time off.

Many Fractional CMOs fall into the trap of becoming constantly available to the client. Obviously, working without a break isn't sustainable and can prove detrimental both for you and the client.

That's why the first consideration should be when you can have some time away.

As a fractional CMO, you might not work with a client every day or even every week of the month. Still, you should have the foresight to balance your time working with an appropriate time off.

The next consideration is travel expenses.

If you're traveling to see the client, you shouldn't pay for those expenses, and your proposal should state that clearly.

Of course, those expenses should be reasonable. You'll be most aligned with your clients if your travel doesn't include first class airfare.

I'd rather spend that extra money to generate results for my client than pay to have a six-inch wider seat on an airplane. However, I'd still expect to have my travel expenses covered.

Besides travel expenses, you should also include your *per diem* or daily expenses. The same principle applies here: keep your per diem reasonable, both concerning your daily needs and the client.

Your proposal should also state that any additional tools aren't included in your fee.

If you require certain tools like keyword research apps, those should be in a separate budget. The value you provide doesn't include the cost of the tools you use. You're not the implementer but a strategist and a leader. You're not paying for hosting or domains either.

This is another often overlooked aspect that should be addressed right from the start. The main things you're providing to your client are your leadership, time, and insights. There should be no expectations of you to provide any paid tools for the team.

Next, you'll want to outline your boundaries in the contract.

If you want to feel good working as a Fractional CMO, you want to be fairly compensated for the work you do. If you continually over-deliver while your compensation stays the same, you run the risk of growing frustrated with the client.

Create a contract you'll be able to execute to everyone's satisfaction. Include the time of day after which you won't be available for contact, such as nights, weekends, or any other periods when you won't be reachable.

Boundaries are paramount for Fractional CMOs. If you leave them out of the contract, you're exposing yourself to potential frustration when your work with a client gets out of control.

For example, if you don't have boundaries outlined, a client might text you at 7:00 p.m. on a Friday. And if you message them back, you'll establish a pretty porous boundary. You'll be saying that they can text you anytime and you'll do work for them.

Of course, if there was an emergency, you'd probably jump right in to support your client. But that doesn't mean you should be available for work around the clock.

On a similar note, if you expect more compensation for any extra work you do, you should write that into your contract as well.

Finally, you should specify your payment terms.

A model I always recommend to every Fractional CMO is to get paid upfront every month. This way, you can avoid collecting after the fact and chasing after clients if something happens and you have to break ways.

When you get paid upfront, you can refund an appropriate part of your fee if you end up canceling the contract. This puts you in a much better position than asking the client to pay per your invoice.

I learned this from the marketer Dan Kennedy years ago. He said, "Rich people get paid first."

Getting your contract right the first time will be hard to do. You'll likely need to do some fine-tuning to get everything just right. The general idea is to write only what you want to do and be incredibly clear and direct about it.

Audition Clients

When I started out, a friend of mine told me I was a golden retriever. I was so hungry for new projects that I would jump at every opportunity, just like a golden retriever would rush after a ball wherever you throw it.

Those days are long gone for me, and the same should apply to you.

Think about your experience, capabilities, and all the incredible things you've done so far. Look at the impact you've made in your clients' lives and the products or services you've sold. Consider the time you've spent working as an employee, consultant, or contractor.

When you reflect on your day-to-day life as a marketer, you'll realize a crucial thing:

You're pretty awesome and kind of a badass.

Naturally, you might not be amazing at everything, but your experience and expertise make you the prize. You're not a golden retriever that keeps fetching the ball back and forth every day.

Why am I telling you all this?

Because you're elevating yourself to the role of CMO, the most esteemed role in all of marketing. And as such, you should stop taking any business you can get.

You need to position yourself as the prize and audition clients to work with you.

You might've started from the idea of selling to people from your pipeline. But that notion needs to evolve.

You want people to *want* to come to you and work with you. You want clients to knock on your door and ask, *"Can I please hire you?"*

This is a paradigm shift that changes everything about your career. Once you adopt the new paradigm, the actual process of auditioning clients will be relatively simple.

The idea of auditioning clients comes down to having an initial call with your prospects and hearing what they're up to without trying to sell anything.

You bring the client on a call and hear about the problems they're facing and where they want to go. Then, you can decide whether you can help them. The clients you'll want to work with will be those who have a big vision, a capable team, and can pay your bills with ease.

The call itself should be relatively short—no longer than 20 minutes. During the call, you'll only need to follow a simple script.

Start by connecting with the client and building rapport. Next, you can question them and get to understand who they are and what they want. Finally, you should see if it makes sense for you to work with that client or send them in a different direction.

This approach fundamentally changes your position. You're not begging for work or asking if your pricing meets the client's budget. You're not asking for the sale in the first call. You're calling the shots and telling them that you can talk more if they fit your criteria.

In fact, you won't even mention pricing during this call. How could you establish a price point if you don't know all the relevant details about the company?

Auditioning your clients will elevate your position of authority and allow you to make the best possible choice. Then, if they qualify, you can move on to a second call, which you should schedule at least a day after the initial call.

Your goal should be to understand your client's business intimately. By auditioning clients, you're ensuring that you're the right fit for each other.

You're simultaneously creating great opportunities for yourself and helping the client in the best way possible.

Use the Simple Sell

Your auditioning call should serve as the perfect setup for closing the prospect. It should lead to what I call the simple sell. That's the process where the prospect sells themselves to you, not the other way around.

The simple sell takes place during the secondary call that you schedule if the prospect qualifies.

This second call can be a longer one, up to an hour or more. I love to start the conversation by offering to ask the client a couple of questions before handing the call to them to ask questions of their own.

You should be radically curious about the company. Ask about where they are in the market, what their team make-up is, and where they want to be in the following years.

The beauty of this method is that you never pitch anything. Instead, the client will likely ask you about working together and your pricing once you turn the call over to them. This will make the conversation much more profound than the usual sales call.

Once the client has answered all your questions and you get a good understanding of what they're about, ask them what questions they have for you.

Directing the conversation this way will signal that you're helpful but not needy. With that statement alone, you'll let the prospect know that you don't need to close that business.

Naturally, you should be prepared for every question the client asks you. If they ask how you can help them, describe the role you'd have as a Fractional CMO in their organization.

Finally, the prospect will ask you about the cost of your services and when you can start. And that's the great thing about the simple sell principle. You won't need to push the pricing issue yourself.

Instead, you'll lead the client to ask the right questions and simply be responsive to them.

This entire process works well because it functions according to the number one rule in negotiation: you have to be okay with the other person saying no.

When you audition clients and let them arrive at the matter of price themselves, you're showing that you're okay with them saying no. Of course, the way you actually feel about it might be different. You might get super frustrated after the fact. But the crucial thing is not to present yourself as needy.

Maintaining this attitude during the call is crucial.

You might be talking to a client that could change your life, allow you to leave your job, and bring in a lot of extra money for your family. But the prospect can never feel that in your conversation.

Similar to accepting a client's rejection, you have to be ready to say no to prospects who are a bad fit.

Rejecting ill-fitting clients will put you in a position where you'll attract better companies. As a result, you'll fill your time working with great clients that you love, and you'll be looking forward to it every day.

Cautionary tale: If you take on a less-than-ideal client and provide a great outcome for them, you'll get referrals from their network. These referrals can often be similar to the client, meaning they're below your ideal. You can quickly find yourself with a pipeline full of low-quality prospects that eat your time.

Bonus Tip

How to Win Clients on the Side as a Full-Time Employee

As a full-time employee, you might consider leaving your job for a number of reasons. Perhaps you've fallen out of love with the company's mission, or there's been an executive leadership change and you are not vibing with your new CEO. Or maybe you love it all but feel you aren't compensated sufficiently.

I used to do plenty of high-level consulting at a marketing agency. While the work suited me, I noticed that I brought home less than 50% of the fee charged to the client. Inevitably, this fact turned my work into a frustrating grind.

I wanted to take control of my own income. This didn't mean I wanted to work with twice as many clients—I just wanted to get paid fairly for my work. And that was precisely what the clients were already paying.

Becoming a Fractional CMO is a great way to do just that. However, there's a risk involved in leaving a full-time job.

But what if I told you there was a way to make that transition smooth and without risk?

You see, you can be a Fractional CMO and have one client. In normal circumstances, this would be very dangerous. Yet, you can do it *while still being employed full-time.*

If you're only starting to dabble in the world of Fractional CMO, there's no reason not to go prospecting and get your first client right now.

Chances are you already know someone who would hire you for a couple of thousand dollars monthly. You would get a chance to see the possibilities of this line of work without risk.

Imagine working a nine-to-five job on the east coast. You get home at 5:30 and, once a week, jump on a call with your Fractional CMO client who's on the west coast. You would get to "try on" the role of Fractional CMO without any risk to your full-time gig.

And it gets better. You can continue to set the stage for your entrepreneurial business until you're ready to go all in.

During my time at the marketing agency, I made plans to leave. Instead of simply putting in my notice and hoping I could eventually build a sustainable business, I started taking clients on the side.

I worked nights and weekends to find prospects and build my network. I also talked to friends to see if they could refer me to a potential client. And that's precisely what happened.

My first fractional CMO gig came through a friend, and it changed my life.

When I made the sale, the relationship with my agency shifted dramatically. I was able to cut back on the low-value work I did before, but I didn't leave my job straight away.

Instead, I kept working on my network. The last thing I wanted was to get back on the open market, resume in hand, and compete with everyone else. I wanted to build a reputation and make people come to me.

That's precisely what happened for me, and it started with a single client on the side.

And the same can happen to you.

If you're interested in becoming a Fractional CMO but aren't ready to leave your full-time job, just remember you can start by doing both.

And when you land your first client on the side, you'll experience the greatest shift in your career.

Taking Ownership to Win More Sales

As an entrepreneur and Fractional CMO, you'll find that many responsibilities fall on you.

If you want to get more leads, convert them into clients, and close deals with confidence, you'll need to rely on your own resources and capabilities. You must own the entire process.

As daunting as that might sound, there's no reason why you can't manage all that. You can follow a simple framework to set up and engage with your list of leads. Then, you can apply the methods discussed here to get the leads to chase you.

When you get to a point where you're having sales calls with potential clients, everything will become easier and start to flow naturally. You'll be equipped to keep your funnel full and make more sales.

And that will be the perfect starting point for your career as a Fractional CMO.

However, it will take more than that to achieve success. You'll need to learn what being a leader means and how you can step into that role.

That will be the very subject of the following chapter. Take a look at LC's journey to building her Fractional CMO practice and how she confidently won clients.

She Won Her First 5-Figure Client in 35 Days... Then 2 More!

If you don't have a marketing degree, I think you're going to love LC's story.

LC is sharp. Though in her career, she has never taken a traditional marketing class. Yet today, she serves multiple clients as a Fractional CMO, where she is building and accelerating her client's go-to-marketing strategies.

When LC joined the CMOx Accelerator, she and her agency partner had never served as a Fractional CMO. They had served clients with marketing projects, such as branding and messaging, but never in growth marketing.

Knowing that her ability to generate big results for her clients was the single lever she could pull to increase her income dramatically, LC set out to solve bigger problems as a Fractional CMO.

Within the first 35 days of joining the Accelerator, LC won her first 5-figure-a-month Fractional CMO client. The client needed a growth-focused strategy, including PPC and SEO. Problem was, LC didn't have much experience in these realms.

Inside the Accelerator community, she posted her questions. Our team and CMOx Accelerator members recorded her videos and helped her see her blind spots. We introduced her to the PPC vendor she hired for her client. We helped her simplify KPI reporting so she could be focused and drive great results.

Within the next 3 months, LC won two more 5-figure-a-month clients. This time, she felt much more confident as a Fractional CMO and has made a big impact for them.

93

Here's what she said:

"Had I joined a year ago, my career trajectory would have been totally different. I wish I had access to this Accelerator 10 years ago."

In the end, it doesn't matter if you have an MBA (or a degree in environmental policy, like me). What matters is that you're committed to your growth, that you elevate to solve the biggest problems in marketing for your clients, and that you get the support you need to see your blind spots and bring in great talent to fill your gaps.

That's what LC did, and that's what you can do too.

CHAPTER 6

Service and Delegation Confidence

"In life, it is never the big battle, the big moment, the big speech, the big election. That does not change things. What changes things is every day, getting up and rendering small acts of service and love beyond what's expected of you or required of you."

This quote from U.S. Senator Cory Booker rings true for most things in life, including the life's work of a Fractional CMO. Success in this profession requires more than just knowing how to win clients. After all, it's how you *serve* those clients that will matter in the end.

And, as a Fractional CMO, there are three distinct things you absolutely need to learn in order to successfully serve your clients:

- Leadership
- Strategy
- Delegation

In this chapter, we'll dive deep into these three components of your success. I'm going to teach you how to create a comprehensive and accurate die-on-the-hill marketing strategy that best fits your clients. We'll also talk about how you can increase the impact you're able to make in a business, as well as improve your team's confidence and satisfaction, all by knowing how to delegate.

But let's start with the first thing on your to-learn list—assuming and owning the leadership mantle.

I. Stepping into the Role of a Leader

Being a fractional CMO means you're the leader of your client businesses' marketing departments. However, from what I've observed in the industry, a lot of Fractional CMOs (and CMOs!) still get confused about what marketing leadership really means.

To clear up any confusion, I'll start by saying that the Fractional CMO is not supposed to be the person who:

- Deeply understands every single marketing campaign and tactic
- Can estimate every single outcome perfectly
- Is the expert in everything

Instead, you are supposed to step into your role as a leader, and:

1 – Understand marketing strategies and tactics from a high level

Your job is not to immerse deeply into the nitty-gritty of each marketing tactic. Instead, you need to see how these tactics fit into the bigger puzzle. By overseeing marketing campaigns from a high level, you can gain a better perspective on whether or not the strategies are working, and can recalibrate your tactics, whenever necessary.

2 – Surround yourself with experts

You shouldn't try to be an expert in everything—that's just impossible.

My advice?

Well, there's this common idea that you have to strengthen your weaknesses. However, for the most efficient use of your time, I say identify your strengths from the get-go. And then, hire your weaknesses.

There are a lot of people in the world who are experts in the things you're not good at. So, instead of trying to get better at the things that are not within your forte or expertise, just find your way to the people who do those things best.

3 – Champion the team to a collective victory

When I hired a marketing technician to serve one of my clients, one of the first things he shared with me on our monthly check-in was just how aligned the entire team was. He felt empowered to drive outcomes for the company and was thrilled to be surrounded by other great people.

In his first quarter with the team, he created a bigger outcome than he was able to do the year before at his previous employer. That feels good to *everyone*—the CEO, the marketing team and you.

Now that you have realigned with what a marketing leadership role entails, I want to briefly discuss a tough subject:

Why Some CMOs Are Uncomfortable Being Leaders

"With great power comes great responsibility."

This may be cliché, but some CMOs are uncomfortable with stepping into their role as a leader because of its concomitant responsibility.

See, as a CMO, you're 100% responsible for every outcome in the marketing department. And those outcomes won't always be great. At times, you'd have to personally take the heat for a huge or embarrassing mistake so you don't pass the heat on to your team.

Here's an example.

Say someone on your team emails the wrong contact list and a bunch of customers mistakenly receive a discount message. And since your client company can't really afford to give out all those discounts, they now have a customer service nightmare on their plate. In effect, arrows will come raining down on the team that made that mailing mistake.

Now, it doesn't matter which member of your team actually had a hand in that emailing fiasco. Your job is to stand in front of the whole team, take those arrows yourself, face the executives and say:

"You're right. We screwed up. I let that happen on my watch. It's my responsibility, I'm going to go fix it."

You have to do that because if you pass the heat directly onto your team, they're going to start worrying about their job safety. That's a huge problem. Do you really want people on your team that are scared to death that they can lose their jobs anytime? Are you willing to let their head go into that place while you're expecting great work and great results from them?

I know I'm not. I'd much rather take the heat, the arrows, and the criticisms before I turn around and work with my team in ensuring the same mistake doesn't happen again.

It takes maturity to be able to take on this much responsibility, which is why some CMOs are uncomfortable being leaders.

However, the faster you can step into your own power and responsibility as a Fractional CMO, the faster you can reach success in this industry.

What Leading a Marketing Team Entails

We've discussed the metes and bounds of your job as a Fractional CMO and why it's important that you own your position as the leader of your marketing teams.

At this point, I'd like to run you through what leading a marketing team actually requires from you.

1 – Focusing Your Team

In order to lead your marketing team, you need to first focus the team.

Remember this: when you have a team that works hard every day but doesn't necessarily know what to do, there's a leadership problem that you must address.

Your team should know precisely what has to get done every single day, even before they show up for work. You don't want them coming up to you every morning to ask: *"What do I need to do today?"*

Their quarterly outcomes should already be explicitly clear to them every quarter. The team member should then break down the outcome into milestones. Every morning, each team member must know where they need to be focused to achieve their next milestone and to achieve their quarterly outcome.

If you don't provide clear outcomes, your team will just do whatever is seemingly the most urgent task, or whatever the CEO just talked about, or something that a competitor is doing. And the moment they start playing this game of being reactive instead of proactive, your marketing department will be spastic at best.

On the other hand, if you can focus your team on solving the biggest problem in the organization within a certain timeline (quarterly), they'll know what their quarterly outcomes should look like. In effect, they can surmise what it is that they need to do by the end of the day in order to keep track.

2 – Giving Praise

Earlier I discussed how, as a Fractional CMO, you need to take the arrows, the heat, and the criticism when they come. Now, what if the outcomes are great and there are heaps of praise coming towards the marketing department? What should you do now?

Well, you do the opposite of what you do with criticism.

This time, you step aside and let all that light shine on your team members. Talk them up to the executives and give credit to how great they are. That's how you end up with highly motivated team members performing at their best.

3 – Establishing Boundaries

There are a number of different boundaries for you to set.

First up: *When do you work?*

As a Fractional CMO, you would likely be working for more than one organization at a time. That's one reason why it's so important for you to be setting up boundaries with each client you're handling, and why you should hold your team and co-executives to those boundaries right from the start.

Do you work every day for your clients?

Do you only work every Wednesday?

Are you only available on certain meeting times?

Establish those boundaries and make sure everyone in your team knows them.

Make sure you also hold yourself to those boundaries.

Because if you don't, and you start replying to work-related emails on days when you shouldn't even be working, people will start to doubt your boundaries, and will soon forget they even exist. And then you're left working round the clock, when you should really just be working for each client *fractionally*.

Second boundary: *How does the team communicate with you?*

If you make yourself available for support communication across multiple channels, you'll eventually find it hard to keep track of all the requests. And when you miss out on those requests, you'll lose the trust of your team.

So, make sure everyone in your team is on the same page about how they're supposed to communicate with you. Is it through Slack? A specific help desk support software? Or perhaps exclusively through email?

Pick one or two channels to really focus on so you can make the commitment that as long as your members reach out to you there, you will 100% reply to their messages.

Third boundary: *How do you communicate with your executives?*

Do you exclusively send email updates every other week to your executives?

Can they send you texts any time?

Set those boundaries to what makes sense for you.

Fourth and last boundary: *What are the agendas for your calls?*

It's so expensive to have team calls, not just in resources but in *time*.

You've got to have focus over team calls, or they will just go on and on and on, wasting everyone's time in the process.

So, have a clear agenda for every team call, put it in the calendar invite, make sure everyone is aware of the agenda, and then drive that call to completion without going off-agenda. If there are other matters that arise during the call, set them as an agenda point for another call. This is how you make your calls aligned, efficient, and effective.

4 – Knowing When to Fire Someone

Another facet of being a great leader is knowing exactly when to let someone go—and when not to.

I am of the belief that there are the right people. And then there are the right seats on the bus. I've worked with people for many years in different companies, that to me are the right people. They're great vendors, they're great team members, I just really liked them. But they've sometimes been in the wrong seat.

For example, someone may be in a management seat, but they're not a good manager, but they're a really good marketing technician. They're really good at piping together different marketing software. So, what I want to do is to take that person and move them to a role where they're going to be successful.

There's a difference between firing someone and changing their job, because maybe someone who's been underperforming is just on the wrong bus seat, when they could be thriving somewhere else.

So, how do you know when it's actually time to fire someone?

Every month, you should evaluate all team members on how well they live the company's core values and if their work product is sufficient. From there, you move to a three-strike policy. If they make three egregious mistakes that demonstrate that they aren't committed to the values of the organization and are unwilling to change, then it might be time to let them go. Be quick to fire bad apples because they can often spoil the entire team in short order.

In the end, gaining confidence in your role as a leader boils down to setting boundaries—what you can and can't do, when you can and can't show up, and who you can and can't work with. Setting all these boundaries will allow you to build a more fulfilling and lucrative career as a fractional CMO, exactly like Russ did in the following story:

How Copywriter Russ Reynolds Plugged into CMOx and Built a More Lucrative, Fulfilling Career in Just 7 Days

One of the most valuable marketing skills is that of the copywriter. Copywriters pen the words that get people to run for their wallets... pull out the credit card... and actually buy something. If I were to rank the most important roles in marketing, a copywriter would be the penultimate role.

That's exactly where Russ Reynolds had ascended. He was a well-paid copywriter who served his clients by writing new marketing controls. He has been the secret weapon of many top direct response organizations and has established a name for himself.

Ultimately, though, Russ wanted more, as he shared with me recently...

Russ confided that while he was very effective at writing copy and focusing on a single promotion...

Oftentimes he would create a larger marketing strategy in order to find additional work with a client. At some point, Russ realized strategy is even more critical than good copy. And that he was giving it away for free!

That's when Russ decided that he wanted to become a Fractional CMO. So, he joined the CMOx Accelerator. Just a week later, he was able to convert one of his copywriting clients into a Fractional CMO client.

But he didn't stop there. By tapping into his existing and previous client database, Russ quickly landed more clients. And 10x'd his investment in the Accelerator in less than 60 days.

While Russ loves that he's now getting paid well for something he used to give away... he also loves being in the company of other great marketers.

"I'm pretty well versed in performance marketing," says Russ. "But the other members of the group have different skills. And we all piggyback on each other—for the ultimate benefit of our clients."

Once Russ landed his first Fractional CMO client, the next problem arose—how best to serve them. And to start the new relationship off on the right foot. As it turns out, that problem was easily solved.

By adopting the CMOx Accelerator SOPs (Standard Operating Procedures) and following the meeting cadence and structure— Russ immediately built trust with his clients.

He was able to take his new client's ever-shifting priority list and turn it into a relaxed yet well-oiled machine. One where all team members were excited about the strategy Russ created and were committed to a successful outcome.

On CMOx Accelerator coaching calls, Russ would learn about a piece of software, a tool, a tip or a trick and would be able to bring it back to his clients, often that same week. Those "hacks" let Russ deliver more value faster, and with less stress.

What I love about Russ's story is that by all measures, he had a career as a copywriter for life. He is well-known for the work he's done and could easily continue to find more work as a copywriter. But that wasn't what he wanted. Russ wanted to ascend to the role of Fractional CMO, get paid for the marketing strategy, and help his clients more holistically grow their companies.

So, if you're a tactical expert—a media buyer, a funnel builder, a copywriter—and you want to increase your rates and produce better outcomes for your clients... book a call with our team at CMOx.co/grow

II. The Functional Marketing® Framework

Apart from great leadership skills, a successful Fractional CMO must have a game plan—a strategy.

There are a lot of people in the world who are happy to call themselves a Fractional CMO, but they're not process-driven people. As a result, they don't follow a process that can produce predictable results.

Now, let me ask you this:

When you hire a therapist…

A personal trainer…

Or any kind of service provider in your life…

Do you want them to have a well-established process that can get you predictable results?

Or would you be fine with them making everything up as they go?

I know I'd rather have the predictable process and the predictable results—and so would all your clients.

That's why I'd like to introduce to you The Functional Marketing® Framework.

This framework is the predictable process you can follow when leading an organization. **It is your operating system as a CMO.** And as long as you follow it, you will be able to predictably produce results for your clients.

But the main outcome you can get from following The Functional Marketing® Framework is that you'll be able to build a "die-on-the-hill" marketing strategy. This is a strategy that's so good, you're willing to die on that hill because any other marketer worth their salt could come in, challenge it, and then end up agreeing that it was the right campaign.

So, what do you need to do in order to produce an incredible, die-on-the-hill marketing strategy? Well, there are three steps you need to take:

Step 1: Understand what your prospects have

To produce great results, you should first know what it is that you're working with. So, find out what marketing assets your clients have. These could include:

- Mailing lists
- Webinars or podcast episodes they've done and recorded
- Books, eBooks, and special reports they've written
- Projects they've abandoned or shelved temporarily
- Any other content they've produced and can possibly be repurposed

You need to audit all these assets and figure out which ones are available for you to use and leverage.

Step 2: Determine what's working in the market right now

You cannot come up with a die-on-the-hill marketing strategy if you don't know which strategies are a big hit in the current market.

So, what's working right now?

Is it five-day challenges?

Is it direct-to-call offers?

YouTube ads? Long-form webinars? Maybe an emerging marketing platform?

Keep in mind that markets continuously shift. New players come and disrupt the scene all the time. And so, you need to have a good sense of what's working in the market—and, of course, in your specific niche.

So, if you're the type of fractional CMO that serves every type of company, this means you're required to keep up with every single marketing tactic across the board to find out which ones work—and which ones are not getting that much traction right now.

On the other hand, if you focus on just one niche, you can likewise focus on finding what marketing campaigns work well for them. Because I'll tell you right now—the marketing campaigns that work well for cannabis companies may not be the same marketing campaigns that work well for financial advisors.

If you already know what's working for the client right now, then you already know 90% of what your clients have to do. It's akin to having an unfair advantage over your clients' competitors—and your own—especially if you're tapped into a community of other great marketers who are sharing this information with you.

In fact, that's one of the things we do inside the CMOx Accelerator. We share what's working right now. We share what user-generated content and what top-down marketing strategies are working. What kind of landing pages and offers are getting great conversions.

So, if you don't know what's working right now, you can just become a student and learn that stuff by yourself. Alternatively, you can join a community where people are already sharing that, and more.

Step 3: Understand your clients' constraints

The third thing you need to do in order to build a die-on-the-hill marketing strategy is to understand your clients' constraints, which can be classified into the three Cs:

- Capacity
- Capability
- Cash

These are the three biggest constraints that typically exist in a marketing department.

Let's start with the first C:

#1. Capacity Constraints

Here are some questions to ask in order to determine your client's capacity constraints:

Do I have the human resource to get the work done?

Do I have someone on the marketing team that can do the actual labor today given the time they have?

Or would I have to find and hire a marketing technician? (More on this later...)

You see, without capacity, you can't make any progress.

You can't simply ask someone who's already working 40–60 hours a week to work even more on a new project. It's not going to happen.

So, find out your client's capacity constraints so we can find a workaround.

#2. Capability Constraints

Say you do have someone on the marketing team who can work 20–40 hours a week on a new project.

This begs the next question: *Do they have the capability to do the work required?*

For instance, you might need someone on copywriting duties. However, it's basic knowledge that some people are writers and some are not. Likewise, the person available might be great at writing copy, but they're really bad at data. This means you can't have them working on dashboards.

In sum, you will still be facing constraints if you have someone who has the capacity, but not the capability, to do whatever it is you need them to do.

Knowing your clients' capability constraints can also help you fine-tune the marketing tactics you'd be employing, at least until you've expanded your team's capacity and have hired a team that can work the full circle of marketing you need to do.

#3. Cash Constraints

In order to successfully run marketing campaigns, you need cash to buy tools, pay for resources, or hire talent. You also have to think about the money you'd be spending on advertising.

You might be working with a company that has no capability but has a lot of cash and they're willing to hire. That bodes well for you. However, if they have little capacity and also little cash to fill that void, then you would be working with a significant constraint that will narrow down the kind of marketing campaigns you'd want to run.

What I want you to understand is that constraints are not there to limit the outcome you can produce for a client. Dealing with constraints simply means you have to be a bit more creative in achieving those outcomes.

The question is *how?*

Well, my top solution to building a die-on-the-hill marketing strategy when I've got capacity, capability, or cash constraints is to hire a marketing technician.

The Role of the Marketing Technician

Later in this book, we'll talk about how you can effectively delegate tasks in order to free up your own capacity as the marketing leader—who is supposed to oversee things from a higher level.

For now, let's settle the issue of *whom* you should delegate tasks to, especially if you're working with a client business that has capacity, capability, or cash constraints.

Personally, in these situations, I like bringing in marketing technicians. They are called technicians because I can't really say from the start exactly what their role and job description is going to be when I hire them to work with a particular client business.

What they're going to do, however, is focus on the technical aspects of marketing and provide support wherever it is necessary. In other words, they're going to be the task rabbit to do all of the labor you need to get done.

If you're working with an organization and they have no one in the marketing department, or they don't have anyone with the capacity and capability to do the work you need for your marketing campaigns, your first hire should be a marketing technician. Even if your client has cash constraints. Especially then, actually. Because hiring one marketing technician can already produce great results for your client's numbers, until they reach that point when they can hire a full-service marketing department.

For starters, the marketing technician can be tasked with setting up a CRM or an email autoresponder software. The marketing technician can also become the liaison between the marketing department and sales, or maybe between marketing and customer service.

The marketing technician is the first key marketing team member, and you can bring them in to work part-time at 20 hours a week, or you may bring them in full-time. Personally, I like bringing marketing technicians in full-time.

Why?

Because I realized that if I don't have a marketing technician in my team, then I'm the marketing technician. If I don't have anyone to delegate the work to, I must do all the work. And that just doesn't work, because again, a fractional CMO needs to be above the daily work, as you would need to run campaigns from a much higher level.

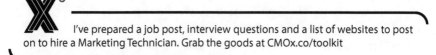

I've prepared a job post, interview questions and a list of websites to post on to hire a Marketing Technician. Grab the goods at CMOx.co/toolkit

Should You Subcontract a Marketing Technician?

This is a question I get a lot, and my answer has always been no.

I don't subscribe to the idea of hiring a marketing technician that you personally pay as your own employee that you subcontract to your clients.

What you want to do is hire someone and install them in those companies you're working with. You want the technician to grow with your clients so they can bring really great value to the organization in the long term.

And you want marketing technicians to learn the way you work.

Why?

Well, because you want them to work diligently every day, full time, to make your dreams come true. Because your dreams are the CEO's dreams. I really implore you to work with a marketing technician you hired yourself—someone you can teach and someone who can work in a way that makes your job more effective.

Now, one route some CMOs take is picking someone who's already an employee of their client organization and trying to convert that person to be the marketing technician.

111

In some cases, this works well. In others, it's an issue.

See, you need someone with fresh eyes coming to a problem. Someone who will take your direction. And someone who will do exactly as you say so they can get the exact result you want them to get.

This would be a very tall order for someone who's already neck-deep in your client's marketing efforts because they just won't have that fresh set of eyes you need. And they might also be resistant to your way of doing things since they've already been doing things a certain way before you even came into the picture.

So, any time you work with a client as a Fractional CMO, you must be able to hire or transition a team member into the role of the marketing technician. As the team expands, you'll have other roles in the company: marketing director, content manager, copywriter, data scientist, media buyer, etc. But to start, you need one person you can focus on the most important outcomes and have them put in the required work.

Know Your CEO's Pedigree

Another important aspect of building your strategy as a Fractional CMO is knowing how to interface with your CEO. In order to do this, you need to know your CEO's pedigree.

Let me tell you a story.

I used to work with a CEO who was formerly on Wall Street. He was an incredibly smart guy who has an impressive knack for details and numbers. His pedigree is that he's a CPA-turned-CEO.

That guy did not care about feelings. Didn't really care about strategy. All he cared about was the outcome, the numbers, and if the cost-per-lead or the cost-per-sale was within his preferred range. All of these numbers are what mattered to him, so he wanted dashboards that showed him the clarity of numbers.

I've also worked with other CEOs who didn't have that same level of detail. Others were more like salespeople. And salespeople solve problems in a very different way than CPAs.

See, if a salesperson needs money, they're going to pick up the phone, they're going to make a sale, and they're going to knock on doors until they get paid. On the other hand, a CPA would crunch the numbers and figure out the best path forward and do something a bit more calculated.

So, when you're working with a sales pedigree CEO, numbers matter, but momentum and action is key. If a salesperson CEO sees a lack of effort (because you're crunching numbers), they might get frustrated.

Alternatively, if you report to a CPA pedigree CEO all about the copywriting hooks you're putting into your marketing messaging, then the numbers-focused CEO may not care as much, right?

The point is that you should always know your audience. Know the pedigree of your CEO so that you can speak to them in a way that actually serves them, instead of a way that only serves your methods.

You have to be able to show the CEO the stuff that matters to them. Sure, all CEOs need to see some numbers in order to gauge your results, but do they really need to see every single number? If they don't have a related pedigree, well, probably not.

Aside from finding out your CEO's pedigree, the most direct way to know what kind of reporting your CEO expects from you is to ask them upfront. Let them describe what they want to see in your dashboard or reports.

From there, you can build a marketing and reporting plan that bends to the will of the CEO. That is your goal as the marketing lead, anyway.

The EARR Loop™

Speaking of building a sound marketing strategy, I'd like to discuss with you one of my big ideas in marketing: The EARR Loop. It builds upon the idea that there are four stages in marketing:

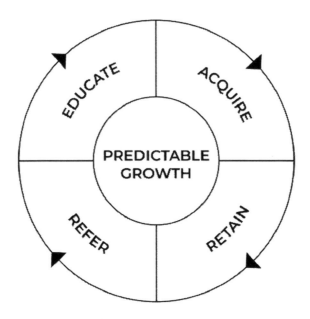

It's called a loop because when you go through all the stages and get clients to **refer** you, then you rinse and repeat the entire process—this time, with a different prospect.

But let's discuss this loop from where it all starts:

1 – Education

When introducing a product or a service to the market, you first have to educate the customer that they have a problem—and that you have a solution for it.

The best description of this is Eugene Schwartz's five stages of prospect awareness. All the clients you'd be targeting with your marketing strategy can be found under one of the following stages:

First Stage: The Unaware

At this stage, the prospect doesn't even know that they have a problem.

Second Stage: The Problem-Aware

The client knows they have a problem, but they don't know that there are available solutions to get rid of their problem.

Third Stage: The Solution-Aware

Prospects who are in this stage already know that there are solutions to their problem, but they haven't heard about your solution yet. They're simply looking for ways to sort things out.

Fourth Stage: The Product-Aware

At this stage, your prospect is already looking at specific solutions to their problem, yours included. However, they're not yet convinced that you have the best solution to make their problem go away.

Fifth Stage: The Most Aware

The final stage is where your prospect is already on the brink of becoming a customer. They know your product, they understand that it is indeed the best solution for them, and they are very close to making a purchase. Perhaps they're just waiting for the right time or the right offer.

So, knowing where your prospects lie in the context of their awareness can help you fine-tune your approach to educating them.

For example, if you run a campaign for a 50% discount on your product, your assumption is that the person reading that promotion is already at the fifth stage, meaning they are aware that your solution is the best one, and they're already willing to buy it—if the price is right.

However, you should also have messaging that targets the rest of the stages discussed above. In fact, your assumption should be that a larger percentage of your audience are not yet aware that they have a problem that you can solve, and that your solution is the best one.

Remember that the more unaware your target audience is, the harder and more expensive it will be to educate them and get them to buy from you. But you can't ignore those who are in the first few stages of awareness, because that is where the wider market lies.

Think of the Squatty Potty. It's a stool that sits in front of your toilet, allowing you to put your feet up and get into a more natural position for using the bathroom. It came out around 2010 when nobody knew that this was a solution, because most Americans never considered that the position of their knees was an issue in the bathroom! So Squatty Potty had to invent the market and created some really incredible advertisements educating the public about a problem they didn't even know existed and presented the best solution for it.

It was hard work and an expensive effort, but needless to say, it paid off pretty well. If the company simply focused on prospects who are already in their most aware stage, then they might not have an audience for the Squatty Potty in the first place.

2 – Acquisition

Now that you know how to handle educating your audience, it's time to move on to the Acquire portion of your EARR Loop. This portion simply answers the question: How do you acquire a customer?

Think through that whole process and come up with all your marketing campaigns in the context of acquisition.

How do you do it?

Do you do a YouTube video to a landing page directing to a call booking form?

Do you acquire customers through email exclusively?

Or do you acquire customers by putting your product on a stand at Whole Foods?

Think through all of your acquisition ideas and make sure you have a marketing plan for each one.

The point here is to amass all possible ideas, not to evaluate them for utility *today*. Freewrite your ideas. You may choose to deploy some of these campaigns first, throw others away, and hold on to a few more for the next fiscal year.

3 – Retention

Once you've got your acquisition plan locked and loaded, we move over to retention. Peter Drucker, who is often referred to as the father of modern management, says "the point of a business is to get and keep a customer."

Getting the customer falls under the acquisition part of the EARR Loop. But keeping those customers requires the retention stage.

Here's another story.

I used to work as the Fractional CMO of a fitness company that sold workout programs at three-month cycles. I looked at the data and here's what I found out:

The company was really good at selling their three-month programs. However, when I looked at the average customer lifetime value, it was just at about 135 days. This means that the average person only stayed on their continuity plan for one and a half cycles.

So, the biggest problem I was poised to solve was:

How do I get more people to stick around to complete their second billing cycle? How do I get the average customer to go from staying for four and a half months—to six months or more?

I thought of different ways I can extend the average customer's lifetime. So, what I came up with was the idea of giving the members embroidered patches. When members join for the first time, they get a patch that signifies that they've just become part of a family. And then at six months, they got another patch that showed their commitment.

And we strengthened this campaign by teasing the patches early on with each new customer. We discussed the patch system with them and gave them ideas, like how they could sew on the patches to their backpack or their hats. There were some reasonably famous athletes who wore the patches to their fitness competitions.

Then, we showed prospects and members pictures of those athletes, which was really fun, because someone who was working out in their basement gym could see someone at a competition who had the same patch. And then suddenly, it felt like the only difference between that elite athlete at the CrossFit Games and someone working out at their home gym is the commitment. And so, members found themselves wanting to stay in their programs longer.

This single idea cost less than $5 per member for the patch and shipping and extended the lifetime value by more than 30%.

Think of some ways you can systematically increase your clients' customer retention effectively. It all starts with keeping your clients happy with the product or service they're getting. And that also brings us to the final R of the EARR Loop:

4 – Referral

When you've got a system that increases retention and keeps clients happy, your customers are going to want to refer your business to friends, family, and colleagues.

However, they can't do that properly if you don't have a good referral process to generate referrals.

The secret to this stage of the EARR Loop is to ask for a referral when the customer is the happiest. Remember that a referral tends to cost nothing. All you have to do is to make it as easy as possible for your customers to create referrals.

So, when setting up a referral strategy, make sure to put it in front of all your customers at certain cadences—preferably when they give you great feedback or when they signify in any way that they're happy with what they're getting from the company you're working with.

Once your referral system is rolled out and it works, you're going to benefit from an ongoing customer acquisition channel that you've never had before. All you have to do is repeat the EARR Loop as many times as it takes to hit your growth goals.

Maximize Your First 30 Days with a Client

Now that you've got the EARR Loop to build your marketing strategy on, you're just about ready to start working with your new client.

At this point, there's one piece of advice I'd like to give you:

First impressions matter.

Your first 30 days working with a new client are the most crucial when making an impression with the team. When you go in and you don't show up to meetings on time, or when you're always late with your notes during that first month, then your reputation will take a hit. And it can dramatically reduce your ability to continue with a client after the first 30 days.

So, you've got to make your first 30 days the best first 30 days for your client's organization.

Now, your first 30 days is really about two things:

- Developing your die-on-the-hill marketing strategy
- Showing your expertise by prioritizing what's most important for the client

We've already discussed how to build a die-on-the-hill marketing strategy earlier in this chapter, so let's take a look at step number two on your 30-day plan:

Prioritizing What's Most Important for the Client

You know what's a surefire way to overwhelm someone?

It's to tell them everything they need to do for the next 12 months.

If you tell a CEO everything the company needs to accomplish in the next 12 months, they're going to get sick to their stomach. They're going to start thinking about huge costs, and they're going to start second-guessing your expertise. They'll wonder if you're even the right leader to do *all* that.

Bottom line is, it's not great for you to tell them everything they need to do in the next 12 months.

My advice?

Build a really robust first quarter strategy. Spend your first 30 days seriously figuring out where the organization is and where they need to be. Map out all the steps you can pull together to make that happen during the first quarter.

To start, go back to your die-on-the-hill marketing strategy. From there, identify the most important marketing campaigns for your client organization in the first 30 days. Then, spend the next 60 days getting two campaigns deployed.

Yes, two.

I'd rather see you get two good campaigns deployed than 50 poorly deployed ones. Marketers tend to play this game of bingo. We tend to say, *Oh, we should do everything*. It's like their measure of success is if they're running as many campaigns as humanly possible.

While it's good to dream big, it's way better to execute something perfectly and focus on getting the biggest outcome for the client over your first 30 days with them.

So, start with holding a brainstorming session with your executive. List down every single marketing campaign you and the client could think of. Everyone can throw out every idea that they have.

Maybe it's conversion rate optimization.

Maybe it's a partnership.

Maybe it's getting the CEO on a podcast.

You can probably list 100 marketing campaign ideas from one brainstorming session. Some of them will be terrible ideas, but some will be a stroke of genius. You don't have to come up with all those ideas—you just have to facilitate that discussion.

Then, in your first 30 days working with the client, come up with a definitive list of which campaigns are the urgent and important ones.

The Eisenhower Matrix

IMPORTANT

DECIDE	DO
Plan when you'll do it	Add it to an upcoming sprint

NOT URGENT ← → URGENT

DELETE	DELEGATE
Remove anything not important	Who else can do it for you?

NOT IMPORTANT

One thing that can help you decide which campaigns to prioritize is the Eisenhower Matrix. Rank the campaigns you've listed based on their urgency and importance.

Campaigns that are not urgent and not important, like perhaps building a new website, may be eliminated from the list. Or the website may be both urgent and important. You must decide.

Special campaigns may be important for the success of the company, but they're not yet urgently needed. That means you can put a pin on those ideas and schedule them on your marketing timeline somewhere down the line.

You'll also have urgent campaigns that are not important. These are campaigns that produce a different result other than driving sales or achieving a needed outcome. So they may be urgent, but they're not exactly of importance to the marketing team you're leading. That means you can delegate them to other departments.

Finally, you have campaigns that are both urgent and important. Tracking attribution, for instance, may fall into this quadrant. After all, if you have a poor attribution strategy, you'll have no insights into the business. Adding an upsell may also be in this quadrant, because you know from your research that a certain percentage of your client's customers would take an upsell. Anything that is important and urgent in driving sales right now should be your priority.

Again, your job in the first 30 days is building your die-on-the-hill marketing strategy, then getting the team started with campaigns that are most important and most urgently needed by your clients in the following 60 days.

NOTE: Inside the CMOx Accelerator, we have lists of all of these marketing campaigns, example success criteria, and strategies around how to get them accomplished. It's a shortcut that saves our members time and allows them to build an exhaustive marketing strategy.

Getting Your Timing Right

As with most things, timing is absolutely crucial in marketing.

From your first 30 days with a client to completing your first quarter with them, you need a certain cadence to get everything you need done within your timeline.

Remember my advice above? You need to build a robust first quarter strategy. And since we've already allocated your first 30 days to identifying your priorities, what you need to do next is to take the rest of the quarter—and break it down into two-week sprints. And then, you attack it.

The 2-Week Strategic Sprint

One quarter is such a long time. You can get a lot of things done over one quarter—so long as you can manage your team's performance, and their deadlines. The two-week strategic sprint can help you with that.

Starting Point	Sprint #1	Sprint #2	Sprint #3	Sprint #4	Sprint #5	Sprint #6	Outcome Goal

The strategic two-week sprint is as simple as it sounds: it simply means you should get your team on the same page regarding what you need to accomplish every two weeks.

Using the strategic sprint, you can rally the entire marketing department around getting specific work done and having a start date and a stop date for certain outcome goals.

Here's an illustration.

When you tell someone they've got 90 days to bicycle from New York City to L.A., there's a lot of vagueness and uncertainty around what needs to be done. It would be a lot easier to tell someone that they need to go from New York to West Virginia in the next two weeks.

Then, when they've reached West Virginia, map out the second leg of the trip which they have to cover for the next two weeks. So, instead of wondering whether or not the person will reach L.A. in 90 days, you can just keep checking every two weeks if they're still on track.

That's your job as the Fractional CMO.

You determine the big project, and break it down into individual phases called two-week sprints. Two-week sprints give your team a lot more focus and pressure to get things done, rather than giving them a full quarter to produce results—which will inevitably result in a lot of dilly-dallying.

A lot of people produce their best work output when given a tight deadline. And that's what the two-week sprint does—it shrinks the time that things have to get done, producing the kind of pressure that precipitates the best results.

But now, this begs the question: *How do you keep folks on track for their two-week sprints?*

The Sprint Retro and Planning Session (SRPS)

Since you're breaking down your quarter-long goals into two-week sprints, you have to hold SRPS sessions at the end of every two weeks. The Sprint Retro and Planning Session is where you get together with the entire team and make sure everyone is on track with their sprints.

My recommendation is for you to do this on Friday mornings, every other week. The Retro part of the SRPS session has three important goals:

- To celebrate your team's wins and boost their morale
- To clarify where the team fell short
- And to come up with the solution to grow moving forward

As the Fractional CMO, you should lead the conversation and make sure you ask the three crucial questions your team members have to answer in order to hit the session's three goals:

1. What are some of the wins you've had in the last two weeks?

I tend to look for about three wins per person. I encourage you to do this, because it's great for a team's morale when their successes are being celebrated. These can include small wins in your team member's individual work or wins where they see other people doing something great.

Here are examples of wins that might be shared:

- We crushed our goal for sales during last week's big launch!
- Edgar did a phenomenal job on the new Facebook Ads graphics!
- We hit our quarterly goal only halfway through the quarter!

It's a great conversation starter that makes the next question a bit easier to answer:

2. What didn't work so well in the last two weeks?

Give your team this opportunity to talk about what made things harder during their last sprint. This isn't a time to point fingers or pass the blame, but just to acknowledge that an issue exists. After all, part of your job as the Fractional CMO is to create an environment where people feel safe to share what didn't work and *why*.

But don't try to solve those problems as you go around hearing from everyone. Just collect them and let everyone share their problems.

Here are examples of things that may have not gone well:

- We had an email go out with a typo in the subject line on Tuesday
- Google Data Studio is consistently misreporting data
- The website crashed and was down for two hours due to a plugin issue

Then, move on to the last question:

3. What are three action steps that we should take in the next sprint to add more wins and resolve the problems we had during the last sprint?

Have everyone write down and share how they propose to solve some of the problems they've heard the team share. After all those ideas are shared, put the proposals up to a vote to come up with the biggest, most important problems the team has to solve.

This ultimately goes back to the ethos of the Fractional CMO, which is to solve bigger problems. In doing the vote, you're leveraging your entire team to identify those biggest problems, and their solutions.

After you've gone retroactive to review what happened during the last sprint, you can now transition into the sprint planning portion of the SRPS session.

Here is where you can lay down what each team member has to accomplish for the next two-week sprint. Everyone should self-assign tasks and outcomes for the next two weeks. Your role is to oversee this process and ask for clarity, or nudge the team member in a different direction if you think their outcomes are misaligned with the quarter's outcomes.

An important thing to note here is to not add anything on top of your members' two-week sprint objectives once you're done with the sprint planning. This pulls the focus away from their specific tasks and would inevitably delay your objectives for the entire quarter.

So, make sure that you use the SRPS session to clarify what everyone has to do over the next two weeks so that when the new sprint starts on the following Monday, your team can get to work knowing what they have to do for the next two weeks. Then, repeat the process once the next sprint is done.

If you do this right, you can produce incredible results within the first quarter of working with your new client, therefore improving your reputation and increasing the probability that you'll be retained for the long term. You'll also strengthen the prediction muscle of all team members, allowing everyone to more accurately assess their own trajectory in achieving the quarterly outcome.

If any team member is off-track for their outcome goals, it is the team's responsibility to support the individual. Everyone succeeds together, so build a team dynamic where members are willing to roll up their sleeves and support each other.

The Importance of Quarterly Planning

After you've nailed your marketing strategy and first 30 days with a client and have produced robust results over your first quarter using the two-week sprint strategy, you'll find yourself in a beautiful position where you already have that cadence that will allow you to hit targets quarter after quarter.

So, the next big thing you have to do is to regularly set those quarterly targets moving forward.

What are the measurables?

How many sales do you need to generate over the next quarter?

And what's the acceptable cost per sale?

Then, map out your quarterly strategy based on those measurables.

Say, for example, you want to onboard 1,000 new customers by the end of the quarter.

The next step would be coming up with the marketing campaigns that will make that happen.

Then, you have to go roll those marketing campaigns out with the support of your marketing team.

But the general idea is that every single quarter, you sit down to recalibrate your quarterly plan. The way we do it at the CMOx Accelerator is that our members get together with me and I walk them through developing a quarterly plan for their biggest client. We do it all live, together, on a big call. I mail a workbook to the members that they fill out during a fun, high-energy call and they are able to then present their clients with an 80% quarterly plan.

After you have the 80% quarterly plan, you present it to the client and marketing team and finalize it together. When 80% of the work is done *before* the meeting, you accomplish a few things:

1. The plan is based on what you know will be most effective
2. The team can add their own ideas and you can have a friendly conflict about what the right path is
3. Everyone feels bought-into the plan because they had a hand at building it

When you do it right, your team passes the Sleeping Test: You should be able to wake up any of your team members in the middle of the night and ask them, "What are you responsible for delivering by the end of the quarter?" Without skipping a beat, they'll be able to answer you.

These are the required steps to building a strong, focused, and supportive team which will make it easier to achieve your client's goals.

Work in Public

Typically, Fractional CMOs work remotely. This is great for our lifestyle, but it makes it exceedingly difficult to understand the day-to-day work of the teams you manage. If you had a desk in the client's office and spent your time in the building, you would pick up on important conversations almost through osmosis. You may see the sales team celebrating a win, or a cake purchased for someone's birthday.

These small events can seem like noise when you're trying to produce an outcome for your client, but, oftentimes, these events can be the raw materials to create new campaigns.

For example, in some organizations, running a company anniversary promotion to customers may be the right thing to do during a slow season.

Also, if you're not hearing what the company is up to every day, you may miss out on communication that you should be abreast of.

This is why I've created a Work in Public process that I believe you should have your teams follow.

If you consider a typical organization that uses Slack, there are a few public channels such as #general and #random. When a 1-to-1 conversation needs to happen between two team members, it is often sequestered to a direct message outside of the view of the rest of the team.

When these communications are hidden, there is no osmosis.

Here are the types of channels that can change the way the department communicates:

#announcements – Read-only for all team members aside from those who manage the channel. Anyone can react with emojis but no one can reply. These may include things like announcing new hires to the entire company, announcing acquisitions, new product rollouts, etc.

#resources – A limited channel that shares all important docs and forms in one place. For example, "Vacation/Time Off Request," "New Tool Request," "Expense Reimbursement Form"

Team channels:

#marketing-team – This is where the marketing team communicates. Any major updates, links to ad-hoc meetings, asking for help on a specific task can all go in here.

#crm-ticker – A "ticker" channel can be set up to display all new leads that come in, their associated UTMs/lead sources, what offer they took, etc. This is great to get a sense of the daily pulse of traffic and to see if something is broken. "Hey, I haven't seen any notices here today… Is something broken?"

#random or **#watercooler** – The place to share memes and off-topic things. While this can seem unnecessary, it's best to have a place for these types of communications to be. You may limit your time in these, or mute these channels, but they're still important.

Worker-specific channels – These channels are to "work in public" so that if anyone needs to work with the front-end developer Bobby, they chat with him in his channel **#tech-bobby**. This is better than sequestering the messages to a private message that no one sees.

Role-specific channels – To keep the #marketing-team channel as clear as possible, creating a few custom channels all about a specific project are helpful. In this way, only those who need to see communication about these projects are getting notifications. Examples: **#paid-ads #seo-external**

This may be a small change in your current communication platform, but the benefits are dramatic. You'll be able to see what's happening in the organization, then focus on messages within a specific discipline (paid ads) or relating to a single person (#tech-bobby).

As a fun bonus, you can add custom emojis to your communication platforms, including the company's logo. It helps make the platform feel more tribal, which increases feelings of inclusiveness, without getting lost in streams of unrelated updates.

III. Building Your Delegation Confidence

You've learned how to step into your role and power as a leader.

You've learned how to build the right strategy with your marketing team.

Now, it's time for the third and final thing you need to learn in order to find success as a Fractional CMO: having the confidence to delegate.

An Important Shift in Mindset

Building your delegation confidence starts with an important mindset shift.

You need to stop thinking, *"I have to do this."*

And instead, think, *"This needs to get done."*

One thing I know about myself is that…

I'm not great at doing my laundry.

I cannot for the life of me fold clothes well.

And I hate the feeling of hot laundry steaming up in my face.

My wife hates it too.

So, you know what we did?

We completely removed doing laundry from our to-do list. I don't do it. Ever.

Instead, we have enlisted a laundry service that picks up a blue bag of clothes from our house, then returns everything the next day clean and folded and ready to go in our drawers.

This has saved us a lot of time and anguish—overall a great life hack that might also be useful for you.

What's my point?

Just because something needs to get done in the marketing department, it doesn't mean YOU have to do it.

Leveraging the Best Talent

I want you to think about what I did there with my laundry dilemma.

I took someone who was really great at doing something, and I'm leveraging just a fraction of their time, in order to accomplish something that needs to get done—but I absolutely hate doing. Laundry is one of the lowest leverage tasks in my life and I was able to delegate it completely.

Maybe you're great at doing laundry. Perhaps you thoroughly enjoy it. But you might not get any satisfaction out of following the latest trends in SEO. Maybe you're just the kind of CMO who doesn't care for pay-per-click. Or perhaps you would never want to spend time on social media, unless you're forced to.

Whatever it is, there's something about marketing that you're not great at. Or something that you don't enjoy doing. Nevertheless, that thing needs to get done.

So, what do you do?

You find and leverage the best talent to get that thing done.

And I want you to see delegation as a strength, not a weakness.

Remember that your job as a Fractional CMO is to solve bigger problems and stay elevated so that you can spot marketing problems easily and figure out the right solution for them.

Now, trust me. Almost never is the right solution for you to get better at doing something you already know you're not good at. You don't need to get better at marketing tactics. You just need to get better at how marketing tactics can be leveraged.

And as a Fractional CMO, you can leverage the best of the best to get work done.

Establishing Ownership for Outcomes

Finding the best person, agency, or in-house employee to leverage is actually the easy part of learning how to delegate. Where things usually fall apart is when that best person doesn't get the right instructions to accomplish what it is that needs to get done.

All too often, when we delegate, we tell the other person that we need something done by a certain date. But we don't clarify what it is precisely that they need to do and *why*.

To help out with that, you need something I built called the Delegation Filter. It's a Google Doc that helps you clarify what you want. It reflects the importance of a project, the risk attached in case the person you delegated a task to doesn't accomplish it, and what the success criteria are. Remember that as the fractional CMO, you're able to see things from an elevated place. That means some things that might be obvious to you might not be that obvious for the person you're delegating to.

So, instead of simply telling them about the thing that needs to get done, make sure you also set the criteria that would signal to the other person that they are successful in accomplishing the task. Make it simple and measurable. Perhaps the number of sales they must generate with a marketing campaign. Or a certain number of webinar registrants they must get after implementing the marketing tactic you asked them to do. Maybe even the number of people stopping by the booth you asked them to set up at a conference.

Whatever the metric is, it has to be clearly defined from the moment you delegate the task.

Don't underestimate the value of giving your team members a clear delegated outcome that they have to achieve. That gives them the opportunity to work to solve the problem, to use their intelligence to spend time on solving it so you don't have to solve the problem yourself.

Get a copy of the Delegation Filter and a short training video at CMOx.co/toolkit

Overall, the Delegation Filter is an incredible tool to give ownership of an outcome and to establish a timeline for its realization.

How Close Are You to Being a Successful Fractional CMO?

Leadership. Strategy. Delegation.

We've discussed in detail these three things you need to learn in order to pave the way for your own success as a Fractional CMO.

Now, I want you to assess how far along you are in learning these three things.

Are you ready to step into the power of a Fractional CMO?

Can you build a robust strategy that produces results for your would-be clients?

And do you have the confidence to effectively delegate tasks so you can stay elevated?

If so, then you are as close as you can get right now to being a successful Fractional CMO. The next thing you need is the direct support of a community of generous, successful Fractional CMOs. If you're interested to know how the CMOx Accelerator can help with this, Casey Cheshire's story could help illustrate the kind of help the Accelerator can provide:

From Zero to 3 Clients – Casey Cheshire Accelerated His Fractional CMO Practice

One of the hardest things to do as a marketer is to create a compelling proposal to sell a client.

A proposal that:

- Serves the client
- Sets boundaries to ensure both your success and theirs
- Clarifies the types of problems you'll work on
- ... and is easy to get signed

Former agency owner Casey Cheshire knew this all too well. That's why he joined the CMOx Accelerator: to win fractional CMO clients without second-guessing.

And he did it.

Three days after joining the CMOx Accelerator, Casey won his first client.

Prior to joining, he didn't know what he could or should charge. He didn't understand the scope of work he should sell.

The risk in him getting this wrong was working too much, not getting paid enough, or getting paid too much and feeling like he took advantage of his client. He wanted none of that!

Casey's price anchor was set low. For years at his agency, he would use marketing strategy as a way to win new clients: identify an improved marketing strategy, then sell services to get the strategy deployed.

He also lacked a niche. By serving clients across multiple niches, Casey had the experience of context switching and knew first-hand the associated pain.

By choosing a niche, surrounding himself with other Fractional CMOs on his level and getting focused, Casey was able to bring in over $10,000 a month in recurring business within 60 days. He was able to staff his clients up using the job posts inside the CMOx Accelerator and refer gigs outside of his niche to other members that he can trust.

If this sounds interesting, book a call with our team to see if we can help you: CMOx.co/grow

CHAPTER 7

Expanding Your Impact and Income through Asymmetric Upside

Young people have it good.

A young person can always risk everything for the possibility of huge rewards. They can afford to be recklessly brave to risk it all for the chance of incredible upside. If it hits big, they could change their lives in one go. And if it doesn't work out, they still have the runway in their lives to try again.

Unfortunately, you may not have that luxury anymore.

If you are married, the sole income earner in your household, have kids or family that rely on you, you can't risk everything for the hope of a great upside.

This is why I encourage all Fractional CMOs to get a baseline of $20,000 a month in recurring business before they take on any high-risk opportunities.

As mentioned previously, startups can be attractive to support as a Fractional CMO. They are often eager to get any help they can and will sign a contract quickly, though they often try to renegotiate the contract to have a lower or zero cash compensation and pay a higher fee upon success.

When I started as a Fractional CMO, half of the clients I served were like this.

The painful truth is that *none* of these high-risk, low-pay, incredible upside clients ever amounted to a big payday. Ouch!

So if you're feeling reckless and you want to try to work with companies where you have asymmetric upside exclusively, let me be the first to bring you back to reality.

But don't get me wrong.

Finding a way to get asymmetric upside with a client is a savvy thing to do. I want you to take on these types of clients, but not until you have your financial nut covered and a pipeline to replace your current clients.

You need to set yourself up financially before even considering seeking asymmetric upside from your clients. You need to save at least six months of financial runway. It would be best if you also keep enough for your business so that it can continue operating for six or more months without cash flow.

In other words, you must get yourself in a position of comfort before you start taking financial risk.

One easy way to find out if you're ready for asymmetric upsides is this:

Are you bringing in $20,000 a month in recurring business with a full pipeline?

If your answer is yes, then you're ready. If not, then fix your pipeline first.

Now, if you're reading this and you're laughing at the prospect of living on *just* $20,000 a month, increase that number. And if you think you don't need that much to live a life of comfort, then reduce the amount.

The point here is that you should only start working for companies where you have an upside—if and only if you're already financially stable.

The next part of this chapter will tackle how you can get asymmetric upside as a Fractional CMO. If you think you're ready for it, then let's proceed.

Traditionally, folks might think that the best way to gain asymmetric upside is to work with startups. But the thing is… this is a dangerous game to play.

Let me give you an example to illustrate my point:

Andreessen Horowitz, one of Silicon Valley's most well-known venture capitalist firms, only invests in 0.7% of all the startups that exist in the world. They check every startup with a fine-tooth comb and make sure to put their money into those that they think will succeed.

Now, you would think lucky startup firms that received funding from Andreessen Horowitz have snatched the golden ticket to success.

But that's not the case at all!

Even with the backing of the most sought-after venture capitalist firm, only 1 in every 2,000 startups succeeds.

Now, if you think you are better or a lot luckier than the head honchos at Andreessen Horowitz, then, by all means, work with startups. But I just want to show you that upside is never easy. I don't want you to build a business where you're just shooting for the moon every single time. I wouldn't want you to work exclusively with startups that couldn't pay you in cash. I'd much rather have you have a safe play around getting paid in cash every single month before the work starts. This way, you're always in control of your income. And then you can work your way to having the capacity to help a company that is a little riskier, but you get an upside on that risk.

The easiest thing you can do to achieve that is to look for opportunities to get bonuses. In other words, you have to structure the opportunity so that you're not just paid in cash. So you might say, *"Hey, I don't* *typically do this, I typically charge $10,000 a month for this, but I'm willing to work with you for $5,000 a month cash, and then I want X percent of all sales made over the current run rate of sales."*

What's important to remember is that your bonus is a percentage of *revenue* share and not profit share. In my experience, profits are tough because they are outside your control. And it's best to let the company itself handle the risks involved with profitability including production costs, supply chains, or even how the executives pay for their cars and lifestyle through the business! It's best to stay away from getting a chunk out of a company's profits, even if it means a potentially greater return.

An important note is that structuring a bonus structure works best with new clients. After all, it's hard to ask an existing client to pay you more for the same work.

Another way to achieve asymmetric upside is by getting compensated through equity.

Most people like the thought of being given equity because it means owning a part of a company.

But I have to point out that owning equities isn't always good.

If you're given shares of a publicly listed company, then that's great!

But if you have equity in a private company, there isn't really anything you can do about that. And there's no telling what the equity is really worth. The only way you can exercise equity is on an exit, and if the owners don't intend to sell, you might be stuck with an IOU that you can't cash in on.

Spend 10% of Your Time Fishing for Whales

Once you've won your first Fractional CMO client, I want you to consider spending 10% of your prospecting time fishing for whales.

Whales are companies that are one to two levels higher than who you usually deal with. They are bigger organizations with bigger problems to solve.

Now, I know that the odds of you catching a whale are much lower than catching one of your regular clients. But the potential upside of catching a whale is just too sweet to pass up. By catching a whale, you could potentially get an enormous payday along with a major leveling up in your abilities.

The opportunity here lies in spending just a day or two a month in looking for and catching whales that can create dramatic growth in your business. Do this so that you won't lose out on possibly great rewards while still making sure you have enough to keep yourself afloat. Some of these whales are large corporations and even startups that can potentially give you outsized earnings.

But again, my recommendation here is to get a baseline of revenue first. Once you have that locked in and you have a pipeline that can continue to produce that in case you lose a client, then you can start having sales conversations with new potential clients who can provide you asymmetric upside.

Go and make $20,000 a month in recurring income as a Fractional CMO, and then consider how you want to grow from there.

Inside the CMOx Accelerator, we have an Income and Impact Roadmap that shares the exact steps and detailed training you must take to win your first sale, scale to $10,000 a month in recurring business, and then up to $20,000, $30,000, and the ultimate goal of achieving $41,666 a month; a $500,000 a year run rate. To book your call with our team, schedule at CMOx.co/grow

Surround Yourself with Winners

One of the special things about becoming a Fractional CMO is that you're able to serve as such for decades into the future. You can create a long-lasting business that provides Fractional CMO services in a specific industry that is more than just a one-person consultancy. You can add additional marketers to your roster and build out a Fractional CMO practice that dominates a niche.

Other marketers have to continually reinvent themselves. The Google Plus experts of yesteryear are now onto TikTok or the next hot thing, while us Fractional CMOs continue to dig deeper and build more expertise in the role of CMO.

If you're interested in sustaining your role as a Fractional CMO, then you must do one thing:

Surround yourself with winners.

Have A-Players that you can count on. When you start surrounding yourself with winners, you're able to get solutions for your clients faster, more accurately, and you can work much more efficiently.

I recently regrouped a few former team members for a new opportunity. We worked together five years ago on a project, and because we really enjoyed working with one another and the work products produced were world-class, we stayed in touch. Over the years, we all got better and better at what we did. So it was kind of a no-brainer that I tapped them for a new project. I knew that we all became leaders in our respective fields, and I wasn't going to pass up the opportunity of working with them again.

It was like getting the band back together.

When you surround yourself with A-Players, the opportunities you give them get executed with more confidence. At the same time, you get paid back by being given other opportunities by these A-Players, too.

But I have to be honest.

Not everyone is an A-Player right off the bat. But that doesn't mean they don't have the potential to be a winner. They may have the ability to be coached into being an A-Player. Your role as a fractional CMO, in many ways, is to be a coach. And that doesn't mean you tell people what to do. Your job is to give your people some perspective, to ask them great questions to really challenge them and maybe their limiting beliefs that they have for themselves.

I love finding upwardly mobile, intelligent, hard working people. And I like investing in their success. If I'm working with somebody who has consistently delivered above my expectations, then I will want to stay in touch with them. I want our paths to cross again.

There's this truism that says: *"No one wakes up in the morning and says, 'how do I make this other person's life better?'"* No one does that. We all wish someone did that for us, don't we?

But you can be that person. You could schedule a time to reach out to your dream team, and check in with them, see what they're up to, and offer resources or ideas that will help them out. Create opportunities for your people to level up. Let them know that you're available to help them when they're in a bind or have a client issue and need a second opinion. In return, you can lean on them and ask for feedback and advice.

One of the best hacks in life is just to love and support the organizations that you believe in and love and support the people that you've worked with that have done great things. Why? Because you want them to continue doing more great things, and you want to be around them as they become more successful.

CHAPTER 8

Solve Bigger Problems

Moore's Law predicts that the computer processor will double in speed about every two years. With this rapid change comes an ever-evolving landscape for businesses. A decade ago, we couldn't imagine the connectivity and social media platforms available to us today.

The COVID-19 global pandemic has shifted priorities in businesses. Businesses are now marketing more than ever before *and* have accepted that having a remote team is how business is done in this day and age. This won't change.

As the barrier to starting a business diminishes year after year with platforms like WordPress, Shopify and Amazon, there will be more and more competition.

To stand out from that competition and to attract customers at a profit, a comprehensive marketing strategy is needed.

But the strategy alone is not enough. These companies need a marketing leader to build and rally their team around a central outcome.

There will never be a time when the role of the CMO is gone; the most ascended role in marketing will continue to be one of the most important roles.

At the same time, you've calculated your current Effective Hourly Rate and realized your number is below what you want. You've defined the number of hours a week you want to work, how often you take vacations where you're 100% disconnected from work, and what your income needs to be to have this lifestyle.

You may have considered starting a marketing agency, but the cost of hiring an army of workers and bringing in business month after month is too daunting. Or you already have an agency and you want to find a way to enjoy the work again by doing the fun stuff: marketing strategy and leadership.

You know you want *more* out of life, and you're confident that becoming a Fractional CMO is the answer.

Instead of risking everything, you know that you can start by winning a client on the side. You can bring in just one client and slowly build your Fractional CMO practice. You've committed yourself to learning, growing, and solving bigger problems.

The only thing missing in this equation is you putting in the reps, and you following a proven process that will shortcut you to your desired client load.

When you commit to solving bigger problems, you accept that your future will forever be bigger than your past. You clearly see that your next paycheck will be bigger than your last. That your lifestyle will *finally* be completely under your control.

If that's you, I have a special gift I'd like to offer you.

After spending years of trial and error, over a hundred thousand dollars on coaching and support, long hours of frustration and disappointment, I built the Fractional CMO community I had always wanted. Members inside are funnel experts, agency owners, copywriters, Shopify site builders, in-house marketers for large and small companies, and marketing consultants. Some members had never made more than $5,000 a month before joining the CMOx Accelerator. Others have consistently brought in hundreds of thousands of dollars a year as a marketing consultant or a Fractional CMO.

The thing is, the CMOx Accelerator isn't for everyone. To ensure that we can help you, I'd love to extend a no-pressure call with our team to see if you're the kind of marketer we can help.

If you want to shortcut your time to becoming an in-demand, successful fractional CMO, book a call with my team at CMOx.co/grow

Above all, you have an incredible opportunity to impact the world. You have a choice: to wield the powers of marketing for good or evil. I ask that you support great companies who solve problems for people and that you take care of yourself and your family by charging the rates you deserve.

If you're ready, we're here to help you grow. Go to CMOx.co/grow and let's get to work.